FURTHER DIMENSIONS OF HEALING ADDICTIONS

by Donna Cunningham, MSW and Andrew Ramer

A continuation of *The Spiritual Dimensions of Healing Addictions,* with healing tools for addictions to substances ranging from caffeine to cocaine, sugar to heroin, and nicotine to marijuana.

WIPF & STOCK · Eugene, Oregon

Wipf and Stock Publishers
199 W 8th Ave, Suite 3
Eugene, OR 97401

Further Dimensions of Healing Addictions
By Ramer, Andrew and Cunningham, Donna
Copyright©1988 by Ramer, Andrew
ISBN 13: 978-1-5326-4512-9

Publication date 5/29/2017
Previously published by Cassandra Press, 1988

TABLE OF CONTENTS

stitute for coffee; Essences and stones to help replace coffee.

iv FURTHER DIMENSIONS OF HEALING ADDICTIONS

ABOUT THE AUTHORS

DONNA CUNNINGHAM, MSW, is a licensed therapist of 20 years experience whose specialty is addicted people and their families. She has used the process outlined in this book in group and individual sessions with recovering alcoholics, adult children of alcoholics, and other addicted people. She is also an internationally recognized astrologer with five books and over 100 articles to her credit. Her first book, *An Astrological Guide To Self-Awareness,* has been translated into six foreign languages. Her second book, *Being A Lunar Type In A Solar World*, was cited by *Horoscope Magazine* as "easily one of the more important astrology books to emerge so far in the 1980's." Her third book, *Healing Pluto Problems*, is already in its second printing and first foreign language translation. During 1988, four additional books will be released; three of them, including this one, are by Cassandra Press.

ANDREW RAMER is a writer, artist, and healer. He has a degree in Religious Studies from the University of California, Berkeley, and is a graduate of the Swedish Institute of Massage in New York. He has been channeling for twelve years. For the past five years, he has been doing body work at the Plaza Center for the Healing Arts, in Brooklyn, N.Y., a group practice with a strong focus on working with recovering addicts. His column on past lives has appeared regularly in *Astrology Guide Magazine* since 1982. He is the author and illustrator of *Little Pictures,* a work of fiction for a new age from Ballantine Books. His channeled work on gay shamanism, healing, and meditation, *Two Flutes Playing— Spiritual Love/Sacred Sex—Priests of Father Earth and Mother Sky* will be released in 1989 by Body Electric Publishing.

This book is dedicated to the guides who led and even prodded us through the long process of gathering the material in these two books—including Tayarti, Nindinac, Arrasu, and Red Feather.

INTRODUCTION TO THE 2018 REPRINT EDITION

THE TWO BOOKS THAT you're about to read, *The Spiritual Dimensions of Healing Addictions* and *Further Dimensions of Healing Addictions*, were written more than three decades ago on personal desktop computers that did not have hard drives but rather two removable 5.25" floppy discs. Donna's computer (if memory serves me) was a new Kaypro and mine was a second-hand first-generation IBM, both of which had green screens and hard-to-read dot-matrix text.

Donna and I were living in Park Slope, Brooklyn at the time, and I wrote this new introduction in loving memory of Donna, who died in Portland, Oregon this summer—on her seventy-fifth birthday. Donna was a warm, loving, and deeply generous human being (with a fierce wit and occasional sharp edge) who brought to her life and her life's work an unusual combination of skills as both a therapist and a world-renowned astrologer. Among her bestselling books are *Moon Signs, Being a Lunar Type in a Solar World, An Astrological Guide to Self Awareness,* and *Healing Pluto Problems.* Along with her wonderful research on the outer planets, Donna will also be remembered for her groundbreaking work on and with flower remedies. She brought great wisdom to our wobbly world and will be missed. Please see her website for more information: http://moonmavenpublications.com/.

These two volumes had long been out of print when Wipf and Stock agreed to republish them, and after years of not having read them I was curious to see what they would look, sound, and feel like. With a growing epidemic of substance abuse in our world, with drugs available that are far more addictive and dangerous than the ones that Donna and I were addressing, along with the expanding legalization of marijuana in the U.S. and other locations (which we could not have imagined in the 1980s), and with studies being done on the controlled therapeutic uses of MDMA, mushrooms, ayahuasca, and other substances (which we did not know about, way back when), I expected these books to be embarrassingly dated—and was amazed to discover that they are just as (if not more) relevant today as when they were first published.

At the time we wrote them there were few spiritual connections in the world of recovery beyond the vital foundations of the Twelve Step movement, but today in treatment and recovery settings the use of meditation, mindfulness practices, yoga, tai chi, affirmations, visualizations, and other healing techniques are common—and yet the "technology" we crafted remains a powerful tool for healing and transformation, as I hope you will discover. The use of crystals and flower essences was not common in the 1980s, but today crystal stores can be found all over the country and you can buy Bach and other flower remedies at any Whole Foods Market. In reading through both books again I did find a few places where our language and cultural references were dated. No one in the 1980s called the person they were involved with their partner. We called them our "lover," which is the word that Donna and I used throughout the two volumes. We invited our readers to "tape record" the exercises. Today we would say, "Record the exercises on your phone." And I wonder how many younger readers will know what we meant when we talked about video cassettes being drawn into a VCR.

Reading the books brought back so many memories, of the scores of people we worked with, alone and in groups, who helped us test out the material and refine it. Thank you all for trusting us and for coming to know that beneath the guilt, shame, regret, and pain of addiction is a wise ancient core in search of what we called the right "power tools."

There are challenges to co-authoring a book, but Donna and I worked well together. We took turns writing, channeling, teaching, and sharing the information we received. In the 1980s channeling was still a fairly uncommon practice, but since that time channeled books have been published in great number, including *A Course in Miracles* and Neal Donald Walsch's bestselling books on his conversations with God. I'd been receiving channeled information and sharing it for more than a decade when we began to work with people in recovery, and over the years I've gotten two main responses when I talk about this part of my work. Some people go "Oooh," awed and impressed, while others go "Oy," doubting my sanity. For years I myself questioned the validity of the words and images that came though me, but something happened in the process of finishing these books that changed me forever.

As I said earlier, we wrote these two books on our (big, heavy, clunky) personal desktop computers, which did not have hard drives but two 5.25" floppy discs. When we were done writing we sent off the completed text to our original publisher on (if memory serves me) two such floppy discs. Some time later we got a letter or a call from him saying that the contents of the two volumes had all come through—except that there was a blip in one section of Chapter Four, and a tiny bit of information was missing.

The use of crystals was new then, but I remember that several of our friends used to walk around with an amethyst chip under their tongue to help transmute their addiction—so it was logical to ask our guides if there were specific stones to use for each of the Twelve Steps. That information came through me one night, and I remember quite distinctly writing down what I heard, step by step, then going over the list of twelve stones and deciding to make one small change. There seemed to be too many green or greenish stones, so when I typed up my handwritten notes I changed the stone for the Fifth Step from MALACHITE, which is green, to its close relation, AZURITE, which is blue.

I'm sure that I would have forgotten all about my tiny one-word switch—except that when our publisher told us that there was a blip on one of the discs we'd sent him—the only thing that was missing from the two volumes was—of course—the information on the Fifth Step! I could hear our guides laughing in the background and confessed my little "sin" to Donna. We changed the text back to what I'd originally been given, sent off the information to our publisher—and I have never again changed anything that I've received from a guide or an angel (although I do still doubt what I've been given from time to time). So, in Donna's memory I now turn these books over to you, to travel through and with on your own inner journey, wishing you every blessing as you transmute the past, heal the present, and step out into a new, wise, and more powerfully loving future.

Andrew Ramer
Oakland, California
December 2017

INTRODUCTION

The problem of addiction is a four-fold one, physical, mental emotional, and spiritual. If you are suffering from an addiction or trying to recover from one, we recommend that you have health care for the physical component, some form of counseling or self-help group for the emotional component, and alcohol or drug education for the mental component. This book is not meant to substitute for these much-needed forms of help. Instead, its purpose is to add another component by identifying the spiritual difficulties which can lead to substance abuse and exploring alternative healing tools. It also helps you repair damage to the subtle bodies, chakras, and emotions and to reprogram the habit circuits through such alternative healing tools as guided meditations, crystals, flower essences, and light.

This is the second of two books by the authors dealing with the spiritual dimensions of the growing problem of addiction in our society. The first, *The Spiritual Dimensions of Healing Addictions,* was also published by Cassandra Press this year. We will briefly reacquaint you with the most important concepts in the first book later in this introduction, so that you can begin working with them. However, much necessary material cannot be repeated in detail here because there's so much new information we need to convey in this volume.

While the present volume deals with specific substances to which people get addicted, the first volume laid the groundwork by showing the issues and needs beneath the urge toward addiction, regardless of the substance involved. For instance, there are a series of exercises designed to help you stop the addiction, whatever it might be. You would still need medical help and the help of a group, yet the visualizations help you reprogram the ingrained habits of thinking about the substance, which are so difficult to kick.

We highly recommend that you complete the work in the earlier book as well. The reason for this is that, as many of you well know, it is possible that you would stop using your substance, having gotten so sick from it that you cannot go on. But then you may resort to another, seemingly less harmful, substance to ease your way, only to get painfully addicted to that second substance. Thus many who stop using drugs start drinking too much, many who stop drinking or smoking begin eating too much, and many who go on diets overdo caffeine or start smoking more. Or, you may not turn to a new substance at all, but instead use credit cards, gambling, or sex addictively. Also, AA groups are finding that rarely are younger people addicted to alcohol alone, but instead there are more and more polydrug abusers.

What this means is that the causes and issues underlying addiction are not being addressed. Thus you can—and should—work through the processes in the chapter of this book relating to your drug or drugs of choice, in order to deprogram your habit. But you wouldn't want to work your way through this volume substance by substance as your addictions proliferated. Thus, you also should work through the material and processes in the first volume, which addresses the spiritual needs and dilemmas experienced by the addictive personality.

For example, there is an important section in book one giving you tools to deal with the emotions most addicts have difficulty handling—fear, anger, resentment, and guilt being just a few. In this, they aren't very different from most of the human race—who among us is brought up to be comfortable with these feelings? However, the addict tends to use the substance to stuff down those feelings, and when the substance is discontinued, the feelings are there to be confronted. It is also necessary to cleanse the backlog of accumulated feelings which, unfortunately, didn't go away just because you smoked, drank, or ate something to deaden them. Without new tools for coping with feelings, such as that section gives you, the temptation to relapse is strong.

What, then, does the present volume have to contribute to your understanding of the spiritual dimensions of addiction? Well, there ARE differences between substances, both in their effects on the human spirit, and in the needs that draw an individual to them in the first place. One of the most important dimensions to understand, and which you don't get in other kinds of addiction programs, is addiction's impact on the subtle bodies and chakras, which are parts of the aura or energy body. Chapter One talks about the effects of addiction on these bodies which are as important to understand, nourish, and repair as is the phsyical body.

The differences between substances will be spelled out in the particular chapters, along with some fascinating perspectives on human history and the part these substances played in it. In addition, there is another chapter we simply did not have room for in the earlier volume, but which applies to all who abuse substances. Chapter Two discusses past life patterns and karma and how these relate to addictions.

The Origins of The Material in This Book

This book and our earlier one came about because one of the authors, Donna Cunningham, is a therapist specializing in addictions but also interested in holistic health and spiritual studies. She was impressed with the work of the Simontons, who combat advanced forms of cancer with techniques like visualizations and affirmations. More recently, Louise Hay has been the teacher for people who are trying to use tools like visualization to help people with AIDS. Reasoning that addictions to alcohol, heroin, or other drugs are as life-threatening as cancer, Donna felt that the same techniques could help addicted people. She also read studies showing that regular use of meditative techniques like T.M. and Silva Mind Control helped abusers reduce and eventually stop the use of these substances.[1]

The success enjoyed by the Simontons, Louise Hay, T.M. and a growing number of holistic health practitioners in tackling these life-threatening illnesses suggests that there is something beyond our physical reality which the mind can tap into, a realm where the mind has the capacity to affect the body. Using tools like meditation and visualization, the consciousness can be trained to heal the body and emotions, bringing a new wholeness to the individual.

Wishing to find methods of using this mind power specifically for addictions, Donna asked her friend, psychic Andrew Ramer, to see what information he could get by psychic means. The result was a fascinating outpouring of material on reincarnation, creativity, mediumship, and other spiritual topics, showing their relationship to the problem of addiction and their contribution to recovery.

Important Concepts Used in this Book

Much of the information discussed in this introduction is covered in depth in the first volume. However, for those who do not yet have that book, we are encapsulating the most important concepts here so that you can use this book by itself. Because this book is a continuation of the process begun there, however, we encourage you to start with book one and work your way through to this point, if you can.

It's a main thesis of this book that we're each far greater than the self we know. That part of yourself which is far greater than the small, fearful being we know as "me" is immortal. Some call it the soul or the Higher Self; in this book we call it the Core Self. You may very well come to experience the Core Self and those other states of awareness in the course of reading this book and working with the material, as part of your recovery from addiction.

There are also other planes and other states of awareness besides ordinary waking consciousness. In our dreams we are out of our body in a place where only consciousness exists. It is as natural for us to be in that place as in the material plane, but we rarely remember being there. Called the astral plane by some, it is the same place we are before birth and after death, but at this time in history people have lost their knowledge of that dimension of reality.

Another common method of altering consciousness, of course, is through alcohol or drugs. As we will discover, addiction-prone people are often more attuned to those dimensions than the average person, but have been taught—as we all were—to fear their perceptions of that realm, which is the foundation of their psychic, creative, or visionary gifts. Drugs, alcohol, and sugar are tools to shut off those fearsome perceptions, tools that easily become abused.

The Life Task or Vision

Part of the problem of addiction arises with the individual's spiritual purpose of their life vision. We all come into this life with a set of tasks or purposes, which we generally do not remember consciously. A number of researchers have substantiated this belief. The most modern and scientific of these investigations was by psychologist Helen Wambaugh, who hypnotized hundreds of ordinary people, most of whom did not have any special knowledge or belief in these ideas. She was able to uncover past life memories in the great majority of her subjects, as well as knowledge of that before-birth state we have been talking about, where the life task, purpose, parents, and special experiences are all planned in advance. (If you'd like to know more about the principles she uncovered regarding the life task, you might enjoy her book, *Life Before Life*, published by Bantam in 1979.)

While we all come into life with a task to fulfill, some who become addicts choose a harder task than the ordinary person. Some, in fact, come in with purposes so out of the ordinary that the life is difficult. The addiction often develops as a way of avoiding the task you'd agreed on, which you now find overwhelmingly difficult to perform. In such cases, the spiritual consequence isn't necessarily about the addiction itself, but about what you are avoiding or defaulting on. When we talk about VISION in this book, we are talking about our ability to perceive and participate in the higher reality, retaining a memory, however dim, of our Core Self and our life tasks or purposes. Part of the process of healing is to regain the vision and face the task. Ways of doing this were suggested in Volume One.

The Concept of Power Tools

All addictive substances are power tools through which users hope to gain strength to realize their visions. They are tools, exactly like fire. On a low flame you can cook, on a high flame and for too long, you burn your dinner. One mistake of the prohibition period was that they were focusing on excess as wrong, so they tried to prohibit everything rather than learn what excess is. Addicts make the opposite mistake. They say, "If some is good, more must be better."

Thus, the process of addiction begins when the person has a dream, vision, or life purpose which they see no way of manifesting. Feeling drained of energy, they reach out to a substance as a power tool. It is abused because people who need strength recognize that power. What they don't recognize is the vision these power tools give, helping you see deeply into yourself. "In vino veritas"...in wine there is truth. In seeing deeply into yourself, you open up a window to perception and become aware of your own energy.

Far back in human history, these substances had ritual uses in order to open up that window, generally in a group and on a seasonal basis. They were used only on rare occasions and in ways that weren't so destructive. Information on some of these uses will be shared in the chapters devoted to various substances. People in our culture have lost sight of these rituals, so they go back again and again to the power tool, which they dimly recall was useful. However, no one knows how to use it properly any more, and instead we abuse it. The use of the substance begins as a way of making the dream clearer, yet winds up making it impossible. It is common to say of the alcoholic that drink stole his dream.

Alternate Power Tools

As you well know, chemical power tools don't do the job effectively, due to their side effects. There are other tools in the world that do the same job with no side effects, no damage to the physical body, your thought patterns, or your emotions. You can feed yourself that needed energy in ways other than from a drug, as we will find in this book. Native American tribes did that. Young people would go out into the wilderness alone on a vision quest. The dreams they had would give them a certain kind of power.

In our earlier book on addictions, several chapters were devoted to introducing you to the use of alternate power tools, nonchemical and nonaddictive in nature. The function of a power tool is to alter your brain waves, your regular patterns of consciousness, so you can channel your thoughts through different frequencies of energy and information. Although there are many power methodologies used by healers, such as acupuncture, herbs, and reiki, the three which Andrew and Donna primarily use and have used effectively in their work with recovering addicts and others who need healing are light, crystals, and flower essences.

It's important to understand that flower essences, light, and crystals do not purport to cure addictions, for addiction is a complex problem requiring many kinds of healings on many different levels. Nonetheless, these power tools are very useful in the total process of healing, a process that may also involve health care, therapy, and self-help groups.

A Reintroduction to Light

Of the power tools we'll be using throughout this book, the chief one is light—not light from the sun or a light bulb, but inner light. It's the source of visible light, the life force energy, the essence of pure thought, the root of enLIGHTenment. This is the light many psychically-gifted people see in auras, those colored energy outlines which surround and radiate from all living things. This light may well be the "visual" effect of the life force or the spirit. These energy outlines have been captured on film in Kirlian photography, so there's proof that they exist. The most interesting of these photographs show a great flash of light from a healer's hands while she is working with someone or even thinking about healing, contrasted with photos of when she is at rest. Light, then, has the power to heal and is involved in the healing process.

In the various exercises and guided meditations in this book, you will be asked to imagine light of different colors. It's important just to trust that some part of your being knows how to create that light, just as it knows how to create digestive juices without your conscious participation. You need not see this light in order for it to work, any more than you have to see stomach fluid for it to digest your food. Some people experience this life force energy as movement, as heat or cold, or as sound, rather than as light.

An Introduction to Flower Essences

An important tool used in both volumes is the flower essence, also known as flower remedy. These liquid formulas are designed to combat specific emotional and spiritual conditions, such as fear, guilt, resentment, or a sense of inadequacy. They are derived from flowers, trees, and other plants, distilled past the level of chemical potency. You may be able to find these remedies through a local health food store or New Age journal. There are remedies based on plants and also on gemstones for many fixed emotional patterns which are difficult to eradicate by talk therapy alone, including many of the ones people drug/drink/eat over again and again.

What the remedies are especially good for is repairing damage done to the subtle bodies by addiction, since they work most strongly on the subtle bodies we'll be learning about in Chapter One. These remedies work particularly on the emotions, helping the recovering addict who has used substances as tools for coping with or repressing strong feelings. As the substance ceases to work, or as the addict puts it aside, many suppressed feelings will come to the surface. The remedies are tools for cleansing accumulations of emotions, healing the patterns of reaction which accompany them, and increasing conscious awareness both of these feelings and of new ways of coping with them.

An Introduction to Crystals

Crystals are among the finest of the earth's natural power tools. With a little attunement to them, one can make the same shifts in consciousness as with drugs, alcohol, and other ingestible substances. The beauty and power of crystals can be addictive too, but with few dangerous side effects. Some people may become too spacey from prolonged exposure to crystals, but such a reaction does not compare to cirrhosis, or heart and lung ailments. Stone crystals are concentrated aspects of Earth-energy, each one vibrating on and resonating with a different frequency.

There are many excellent books and workshops available on crystals and crystal healing. It is not our intention in this book to duplicate any of that material, but we do want to share with you several crystal uses that have bearing on the healing of addictions. In each chapter dealing with a substance addiction, you will be given an exercise in which you hold one kind of stone in your left hand and a different kind in your right. The kinds of stones are different for each addiction.

By holding two different crystals in your hands and deepening your awareness into them, letting their energy wash through you and move you, you can create excellent substitutes for addictive substances. The cerebrum of the human brain is composed of two hemispheres. Each has slightly different ways of processing information. The right hemisphere, which controls the left side of the body, is more fluid, spatial, and visually oriented. The left hemisphere, which controls the right side of the body, is more linear, time-oriented, and verbal. By holding a different stone in each hand and working with the pair, you can subtly alter your brain functions and initiate different states of consciousness.

At first it may be difficult to feel the energies of the stones. It takes a certain amount of sensitizing to be able to do that. Let your hands reach out from deep within you. Think of the stones as living, almost like pets. Their vibration may be very slow, but when you hold them and think of them as living creatures, you may find it easier to feel them, more like holding a kitten or a baby bird. Feel that when you hold your crystal you can breathe in its energy through your hands into your body. Because of their structure and nature, crystals are able to retain information put into them, and can carry energy from outside sources. For information on how to select, program, and cleanse your crystals, refer back to the crystal chapter in the earlier volume or to a book on crystal healing.

The Healing Crisis

Once you make a conscious decision to change your life, you may find yourself in the midst of a healing crisis. This is just like that period when you're cleaning out a closet—with things emptied out all over—and it seems that there's more of a mess than there was before. Many who have started on this path have been plunged into further despair through not understanding what was happening. This may have happened to you several times in your past as you tried to let go of the addiction. Do not despair. This period will not be easy, but if you trust the cleansing, and if you keep on cleansing, it will pass.

If the addiction has been to repress feelings, you have to expect them to re-emerge bit by bit when you stop. Just as you detoxify on the physical level, you can expect detoxification on the emotional level as well. The important thing is not to let any of the feelings overwhelm you or get too attached to them—they pass, just as the symptoms of physical detoxification pass. They can tell you a great deal about yourself and the conflicts from which you've been hiding, but they're likely to be exaggerated from being pent up so long. The exercises and tools in our previous book on addictions give you specific guidance on how to deal with several different kinds of emotional catharses.

Feelings may come up from your past—anger, resentment,hurt—and you may try to attach them to something in the present. ("It's not logical," you say to yourself, "to be so angry about something that happened twenty years ago.") For instance, you may suddenly be furious at a lover who left you ten years ago, but you inappropriately direct that anger toward your present lover, or a family member or good friend. You may attribute it to something this person has just done, so you can say you have cause for the anger...but not to that extreme. Be aware of this tendency to displace feelings, and keep redirecting them to the proper target.

Also, don't try to rationalize the feelings away. ("That's all in the past. It doesn't make sense to cry over it.") Don't cover them over with phony forgiveness or sweetness and light. Real forgiveness and acceptance will come later, as you work the exercises through to completion, but not until you've allowed yourself to experience the rage or hurt.

And Now We Begin...

With this summary of important concepts from our earlier book, you're ready to learn more about the spiritual dimensions of addictions...and of yourself. It's important to know that you'll have to be as persistent in seeking out your healing as you were in seeking out your drug of choice. Although this book can give you important insights into the spiritual dimensions of your difficulty, don't neglect the other dimen-

sions. Treat your body lovingly, with the help of your health care practitioners. Look into your emotions, with the help of a therapist, if you need
it. And reconnect with your fellow human beings, with the help of a
support group like the twelve step programs. This book is not the only tool
you need, even though it can give you some important information. We
salute you for your courageous pursuit.

1 You can read about their work in: O. Carl Simonton, M.D., Stephanie
Matthews-Simonton, and James L. Creighton. *Getting Well Again,* Bantam,
New York, 1978. Another illuminating source is Bloomfield, Harold, M.D. and
Robert B. Kory. *Happiness: The T.M. Program, Psychiatry, and Enlightenment,*
Simon and Schuster, New York, 1976. Also see Silva, Jose. *The Silva Mind
Control Method,* Pocket Books, New York, 1977, pp.145-52.

CHAPTER ONE

WHAT THE SUBTLE BODIES AND CHAKRAS ARE AND HOW ADDICTIONS AFFECT THEM

The Energy Body or Aura

In addition to the physical body, we have a number of bodies on other planes of existence which interpenetrate and affect our own. The energy body or the aura surrounds the physical body and, though slightly larger, corresponds to it. The psychically awakened can see, feel, or even hear the aura. It actually has several layers, corresponding to the physical body, the etheric body (an energy double of the phsyical body), the mind, and the emotions, as well as a layer called the causal body which works to bring our visions and thoughts into form. The different layers are known by a variety of names.

These subtle bodies are damaged by addictions. The psychically awakened often perceive holes or leaks in the outline of the energy body of an addict, places where the abuse of power tools has ruptured this sensitive energy membrane. Leaks may cause a puzzling drain of energy or an oversensitivity to the influence of other people. Addicts and those closely connected with them frequently have trouble with boundaries, and aura holes are part of the reason. Also perceivable may be areas of damage—perhaps seen as dark spots in the aura, or felt as areas of abnormal heat or cold.

In your attempts to recover from addiction, these bodies must be repaired along with the physical body, or you cannot return to health. You may even be subtly enticed back into addiction as a way of dealing with the energy blockages or drains. Working on the energy body is part of the practice of polarity therapy, touch for health, reiki, MariEL, and crystal healing. We will also present some exercises here to help you.

EXERCISE: Cleansing the Aura

Follow these steps:

Put yourself in your bubble and breathe deeply until you feel a shift in consciousness.

Imagine that you have a large, thick cylindrical brush—like the brushes used on baby bottles. Imagine that it's constructed of glowing white light.

Divide the front of your energy field into sections—perhaps four. Scour each section diligently with the brush. Then pay attention to scouring the joining places between the four sections.

Turn around in your bubble so that you now face the uncleaned portion which was behind you. Repeat the previous step. Then scour the places where the front and back halves of the bubble are joined.

Use a liquid white light with a jacuzzi action to wash down the bubble. Keep flushing the light liquid down the sides until the liquid runs clear and clean.

Feel how different it feels to be in a clean bubble—that is, a clear aura.

Another tool for cleaning your energy field is a water bath in which you've dissolved sea salt, baking soda, or up to a quart container of epsom salts. You could also burn sage and have someone pass the smoke through your energy field. Finally, a chunk of green tourmaline is excellent for cleaning your energy field. Hold it in one hand and swirl it around through the bubble.

EXERCISE: Clearing Out Other People's Energies

When you are in the public, especially in agitated atmospheres or on crowded public transportation, you can pick up energy contamination. If your aura is weakened by addiction, you can also absorb a great deal of negative energy from people close to you, particularly when they are upset and reaching out to you. The following exercise may need to be done as often as once a day, perhaps before going to sleep, when you've been in public places or in periods of intense interaction with others.
Get into your bubble and blaze up the white light brightly. Put all the people you've come into contact with that day into a big bubble across from yours. (This also works for important but difficult people in your past, such as parents or mates.)

Imagine that you have a big magnet in your solar plexus, and that it's drawing back your energy from all those people. Imagine them instead drawing down energy from their Core Selves.

Imagine that the other bubble also has a big magnet on the outside, and that it's drawing out from you all the energy you've absorbed from these people. If the energy is difficult and you're reluctant to have them reabsorb it, imagine that they have a jaccuzzi inside their bubble which is flushing the energy down beneath their feet.

Now move their bubble behind you, where it is even more powerful, and where it will draw out energy you have unconsciously and psychically absorbed.

Pull down fresh energy and inspiration from your Core Self. Then dissolve the bubble.

EXERCISE: Mending Your Aura

In the course of doing a major cleansing of your energy body through these two exercises, you may have perceived holes or leaks in your aura. The following exercise, done as many times as you feel the need, will work to mend this body. Actually, each time you sit in your bubble of light, you are strengthening your aura.

Once again, construct the bubble. Find places where there is damage— holes, leaks, or maybe just places where it's wearing thin. You may see them, feel the movement of energy, or sense temperature differences.

Where there are major holes, you may first have to use light-plaster to fill them in. Light-spackle will probably do for the small holes and cracks. Do a thorough job of mending.

Now pretend that you have a paint roller constructed of glowing white light and a pan of glowing white light-paint. Cover the roller with light-paint, let it get absorbed into the roller and roll a thick layer of it all around your aura.

Let it dry and then glory in the brilliance and peacefulness of your newly-restored energy body.

The Major Chakras

Centers in the energy body called chakras, almost like the organs in the physical body, govern the subtle senses by which we give and receive information that isn't apparent on the physical plane. They also serve as outlets for giving and receiving energy. At the chakra points, energy flows back and forth between the physical body and the nonmaterial plane, connecting us with the divinity in ourselves and others. Essentially, they're the channels for the vision we've been discussing. As you tune into your chakras, you may sense them as spheres or pulsations of energy about an inch to an inch-and-a-half in diameter.

Visionaries, creative people, and psychics have very sensitive chakras which are easily wounded. They feel everything so keenly that it's painful, and they may drug, drink, or overeat to shut down the pain. People of keen chakra sensitivity are not well-appreciated in our world and may be considered weird. They may feel isolated and turn to addiction in an attempt to compensate for loneliness.

The locations of the major chakras are shown in the accompanying diagram. When power tools like drugs or alcohol are misused, the chakras get blocked, and we come to feel cut off from both humanity and the Divine. We're also cut off from the flow of life force the energy body provides. The abuse of chemicals, even those not designated as drugs, jams up the chakras, fixating the user primarily in the lower three chakras. No doubt, you'll see the source of certain symptoms in the descriptions which follow.

The ROOT CHAKRA, at the base of the spine, governs survival, self-protection, and our grounding in the world. People fixated in this center are often earthbound, inert, and materialistic, while people who have poorly functioning root chakras are often insecure and afraid, preoccupied with the past and the self, and are not well-grounded. They're what is popularly known as "spaced out." Damage to the root chakra, as through a traumatic uprooting, may have a connection to addiction. A number of studies have shown that various ethnic groups—e.g. the Irish Americans or the Italian Americans—have a far higher rate of alcoholism or alcohol dependency in this country than in their own country. The high rate of drug addiction among Latin Americans in New York and other cities may have a similar relationship to root chakra traumas. Other root chakra traumas which may predispose people to addiction are war, the early loss of a parent, having a parent who is severely abusive or addicted, or being in foster care. Addicted people who have suffered traumas such as these can use the exercises given later in the chapter to repair the root chakra.

The SEXUAL CHAKRA, two inches below the navel, governs sexual attitudes and desires. The person negatively fixated there is hung up in sexuality and in the senses, and bases most interactions and perceptions on them. Alternatively, or at a later stage of the addiction, there can be a paralysis of feeling in this area. Traumatic experiences which can damage this chakra are incest, rape, difficult childbirth, or a stillborn pregnancy. Addicted people who've suffered traumas such as these can use the exercises given later to repair this chakra.

The SOLAR PLEXUS just above the waist governs personal power, balance, and self-esteem, and when blocked or damaged leads to self-hate

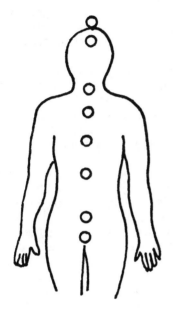

Crown Chakra
Brow Chakra

Throat Chakra

Thymus Chakra

Heart Chakra

Solar Plexus Chakra

Sexual Chakra
Root Chakra

DIAGRAM OF CHAKRAS

and a closely related self-centeredness, or a feeling of powerlessness, and lack of self-assertiveness. It also governs the desire for bliss and the wish for material things. Negatively accentuated, it produces addictive greed wherein there's never enough to satisfy the person. Traumas to the solar plexus include having a hypercritical parent, being an unwanted child, having a bad ego wound such as a rejection in love, or failing in a beloved enterprise. Associated with solar plexus damage is sleep disturbance and the wish to blot out consciousness. The first three centers are the ones most attuned to the primitive parts of our nature, the ones to which we easily become enslaved.

The HEART CHAKRA is a crucial one in addictions, and will be mentioned often in this text. It's located in the same area as the physical heart, and is the true source of sensations such as heartache. The heart chakra is tied to the ability to give and receive love. Wounds to the heart center can include rejection by a loved one or parent, and the loss of a loved one. Growing up in the home of an addicted parent means insufficient heart center nurturing.

The THYMUS CHAKRA can be found in between the heart and throat chakras. We're used to thinking of seven major chakras, but part of our collective spiritual growth at this time is the awakening of this new energy center within us. Some call this point the high heart, the upper heart, the secret heart, or the witness area. It might also be called the chakra of global responsibility. As the heart deals with personal love, the thymus is about our planetary connection. It's the chakra of peace, universal love, and compassion. Whereas the heart connects us with others on a feeling level, the thymus connects us to the rest of the world on an action level. It's related to our capacity to be what we call Peace Warriors. The word thymus comes from a Greek root for spirit or courage.

Will, good will, the right use of will—all are an aspect of this chakra. But the way we use the word WILL allows for both good will and bad will, while the function of this chakra is beyond duality. If someone misuses love, we know that it's not love, but need, control, or possessiveness that motivates them. So, too, with the function of this chakra. It might be called Divine Movement instead of will, until the right word for it emerges in our group consciousness.

The thymus chakra was originally connected with the heart chakra, its next-door neighbor. However, medical researchers have recently discovered that the physical heart has endocrine gland functions that can be tied to the heart chakra as the thymus gland is tied to the thymus chakra. The thymus gland is an important part of our immune system. It participates in the body's knowing what is self and what is not self and therefore not safe, needing to be removed. The gland is large in children and seems to wither as we age. Before the decline in breast feeding, a certain amount of immunity came to us from our mothers' milk. The decline in breast feeding deprived us of this added source of immunity.

This loss may have forced our thymus glands to overwork, and may be involved in the rapid rise of immune deficiency diseases. (Other contributing factors may be routine immunizations to the less serious childhood diseases, which keep the body from developing its own immunities, and the abuse of antibiotics, which also affect the immune system.) On another level, however, these developments regarding the thymus gland and the immune system are part of the process of consciously awakening this chakra. As this new chakra awakens in more and more of us, the thymus gland will become stronger, so our bodies will be able to tolerate far more of what is now reacted to as foreign.

There is still some confusion within us between this newly emerging center, which we sense without being conscious of it, and the heart itself, for this center is a natural expansion of heart energy. Many addicts, because they are front runners, may be opening this chakra without knowing it, which may contribute to their well-known trouble with lack of boundaries between themselves and others. The chakra will teach us new ways of being in relation to everyone else on the planet.

Very often, New Age healers and teachers speak much about love and yet seem distant and cold on the personal level. They may be working out of the thymus chakra, but think they are using their hearts. Likewise, many people who go through physical death and are resuscitated (especially by electrical stimulation to the heart/thymus area) "come back" with an opened thymus chakra, and then suffer from problems in their closest relationships because they now operate more from universal love than from personal love. As this chakra awakens in more and more of us, there will be a balance between the heart chakra function of love as feeling and the thymus chakra function of love as action. Then we will create a global network of mutual responsibility that will carry us to new ways of living in the world that most of us cannot even imagine.

Because the thymus chakra is just opening, it's rarely damaged but rather still non-functional. All addictive substances interfere with the awakening of this chakra. They tend to lock us into our own little world and our own little dramas, which keep us distant from the capacity to awaken a global vision. Part of our healing is to awaken and balance this chakra, to take in and to beam out its frequency. As this chakra opens more and more, your capacity to participate in global transformation will increase, and you may find that the experiences of your addiction are transmuted into that which you'll be able to share and teach.

The THROAT CHAKRA affects the ability to communicate, to speak the truth and do it with kindness. Experiences which contribute to throat center blockages include toxic secrets in the family, or being forced to hide your feelings or your true self, in your family or relationship. When there's a blockage of energy in the throat chakra, the person also feels isolated, not understood by other people, and creatively blocked. Chanting and mantras open the throat center.

The BROW CHAKRA is inside the brain, between the eyebrows where the pineal gland is located. This chakra is often called THE THIRD EYE. It's the seat of mental creativity, the capacity to visualize, and the source of psychic abilities. It's the locus of the mind, the guru within, the gateway to our spiritual journey.

The CROWN CHAKRA, located at the very top of the head, is the point of contact with the Core Self, what is beyond the mind, the source of cosmic consciousness, and our spiritual center. Both this and the brow chakra are opened by meditation. When people say that they're just "talking off the top of their head," they're alluding to the inspiration that can come from attunement to these two centers.

Still More Chakras

In addition to these major chakras, there are several other secondary chakras we'd like to talk about. On the left side of the body but between the solar plexus and heart chakras is the spleen chakra. It functions as an internal energy harmonizer and balancer. Whereas other chakras have strong energy outflows, the spleen chakra draws in cosmic energy, so you may want to attune yourself to it and open it when you need more energy, so that you feel yourself breathing it in through this point.

In the palm of each hand and on the bottom of each foot, there are other centers. Those in the hands relate to creativity, self-expression, and the ways we reach out to the world. Those in the feet relate to the way we touch the earth and move through our lives in a grounded fashion. It's important to explore these chakras and to heal and open them. You can adapt the exercises given later in the chapter to work with these four.

All the joints of the body have chakras too—ankles, knees, hips, shoulders, wrists, and elbows. These are smaller chakras, but you can use the same techniques on them until your entire body is glowing with light. There's also a chakra that floats above your head, beyond the physical body. Some call this the trans-personal point, others call it the star point. As the crown chakra connects us to the world of spirit, this one is a step beyond that. As we become aware of it, we move out into a nondual consciousness that connects us to all worlds and dimensions. This chakra, like the thymus chakra, is seldom damaged, but more un-awakened. So tune into it, feel it glowing, feel it unfolding, a petal at a time.

Chakras and History, Shifts in Chakra Emphasis

As we'll discover in our discussions of various substances, each addiction has its day. So does each chakra. Of course, all chakras must be integrated for a healthy person, but there are differences in emphasis in different eras. Early in our history on the planet, the root chakra was a crucial one as we came to terms with being in physical form and learned to deal with the realities of the earth and surviving on it. We've made progress with the root center, as we've mastered our environment, although it's often two steps forward, one step back—witness the growing problem of homelessness. Naturally, those in underdeveloped countries or impoverished areas of our own land where survival is hard still must devote a large part of their energy to pure root chakra work.

Currently, in this affluent land of ours, our major tasks involve the heart center, in learning to love all other beings unconditionally; the thymus, in participating in the global healing and union; and those still higher in the body. The mass attraction to marijuana in the Sixties came about as we collectively sensed its capacity to affect the thymus. We turned to pot to boost us forward to global union, and made some progress.

Although the addict, especially the visionary sort, may glimpse these upper centers, it's difficult to use them well unless you have mastery over yourself. Few in our culture have fully developed these upper centers because disciplined spiritual practice with tools like meditation are needed and we're not a meditative culture. This is one of the reasons addictions are so pervasive here, since without tools like meditation it's hard to be in touch with your vision and to receive the necessary inspiration and strength to manifest it.

The Effect of Various Substances on the Chakras

Alcohol and the heavier drugs break up the vertical flow of energy through the chakras, along the spinal column. Each addictive substance has an initial affinity with one of the chakras, the first to be affected as that power tool is abused. Fears connected to a particular chakra may have something to do with your choice of addictions. People with multiple addictions have multiple fears. In discussing various addictions, we'll talk more specifically about the chakras affected by that substance. In general, however, the heavier the substance, the lower the center it has an affinity for. Hard drugs like heroin or barbiturates wipe out all the centers and all vertical flow through them. Any addiction, in time, can damage all the chakras.

You should also know that there's a spillover effect wherein the blockage to a particular chakra can result in a damming up of energy in chakras on either side of it. Thus, if the heart chakra is wounded, whether through addiction or trauma, energy eventually gets dammed up in the solar plexus as well, with implications for self-esteem and a resulting self-centeredness. The thymus, being still mostly unawakened, can be even more paralyzed. The throat chakra, on the other side, can also be affected, so that the person stops talking about feelings. If the sexual chakra gets damaged, whether through addiction or trauma, there may be effects on the root chakra or the solar plexus. In general, substances classed as uppers— from coffee to cocaine to amphetamines—jam the energy upward, while substances classed as downers—from sugar and alcohol to heroin—jam the energy downward. When the spillover continues for a long time, there can be a backup to the next few centers up and down the line. It's a lot like a blockage in the plumbing or a short in an electric wire.

This damage accounts for many of the problems common to addicts and those who love them. The self-centeredness, the progressive withdrawal into a smaller and smaller world devoid of human contact, and sexual problems (either impotence or promiscuity) are all understandable within the context of chakra malfunctioning. We'll give exercises, stones, and flower remedies to help mend the chakras later. As the person recovers, also, there are often crises corresponding to the chakra which is healing. For example, there are often periods of unreasoning rage, anxiety attacks, and sorting out one's sexuality.

Addictions and the Heart Center

In the person who hasn't been damaged by drugs or other chemicals, energy flows from the lower chakras up to the heart center and out the heart to others. An exchange of loving energy is set up. When the outward flow of energy stops, the person becomes increasingly isolated and self-centered and can drink, drug, or overeat even more to stop the pain of being shut off.

Addictions are an increasing problem for all of us, and one contributing factor is the virtual disappearance of breast-feeding in this century. The breast is next to the heart, and the gentle, loving stimulation by the baby of the mother's breast did much to open the mother's heart toward the baby and keep it open. Feeding and loving were inseparable— the baby automatically got a flow of love energy as it ate several times a day. No such automatic opening happens with bottle feeding, and there's no energy exchange at all with a pacifier. As a result, most adults and children in this culture have suffered some chakra starvation, some deficit in the automatic learning of how to let the energy flow through those chakras. Never having learned, we don't know how to give or receive it, so all our relationships suffer in depth. We can be taught to open the flow by using the exercises given later.

The damaged heart center becomes a magnet, rather than something that pours out, so addicts leech energy from others in desperate and distorted ways that further twist their relationships. On a subliminal level, the addict perceives that playing on your sympathies will result in more energy as your heart literally "goes out to them." For this reason, addicts can be incredibly draining to be close to or work with, which predisposes them to further losses. When the other person cannot bear being drained any more, the relationship may be terminated. The addict, reeling from still another heart wound, may sink even deeper into the addiction.

Heart center closure is one of the vicious cycles of addiction. In fact, a heart wound can be one of the ways addictions get started in the first place. Many people begin abusing substances after the loss of a loved one. Many young people find drugs become a problem after they leave the nourishment of home, or after home is no longer a source of nourishment.

The children and spouses of addicts are particularly addiction-prone. One of the reasons is that living with an addict brings on heart-center starvation. Still others who grow up in loveless environments or who suffer early losses may also have an undernourished heart center which predisposes them to addiction. In growing up, we learn from those a-round us, and in such households, we don't learn how to let heart energy flow.

Gay people are another group with a high rate of addictions: one in three is an alcoholic and many also abuse drugs. Heart center wounds can play a part in this, because family and friends often reject them when the homosexuality is revealed and because of the ways they must deny or distort their true heart feelings, so they suffer from isolation. Associating mainly with other gay people who have suffered similar heart wounds can contribute to energy starvation. The gay community can reverse this trend by consciously feeding and filling each other's heart center such as by practicing the excercises presented later.

People who "pour their heart into their work" can also suffer heart starvation, since there's no two-way flow—the work cannot give back. Thus, workaholics and those who have to live with them often become alcoholics or addicts. Shut off from other people—in the garret or the office, it doesn't matter—the person gets depleted and drained, turning to the substance to dull the pain.

Even once the addiction has stopped, the heart center problem continues unless there's a conscious effort to re-educate and retrain it. In some, there's a spontaneous reopening in the wake of a powerful spiritual experience or a great love affair. All too soon, however, the glow fades and the heart center may close. For many, however, it doesn't reopen unless retrained. People who have stopped the addiction but not reopened the heart can be miserable, for they're cut off from love and yet have nothing to dull the pain. The temptation to go back to the addiction can be strong, causing many relapses. The healing exercises we'll do later are designed to restore the flow.

Navel Blockage and Addiction

During fetal development and infancy, another energy center functions in the human body, the navel chakra. This is what nourishes us at the energy level, enabling us to grow so rapidly. By the second year, it should have closed down, allowing energy to flow upward to the higher chakras, that begin to function after birth. Thus, the age of two is particularly crucial, and any loss or separation up to that age increases the child's vulnerability. If loss should occur, or if the navel chakra is neglected or overfed, that area may be blocked after the chakra itself closes down, preventing energy from fully flowing upward, depriving the higher chakras and causing problems later in life.

Likewise, when the navel chakra is improperly nourished in infancy, it also becomes over-stressed, and the person looks for relationships or substances to fill the void. In such cases, the heart center hasn't developed properly either, so the person doesn't know how to give or receive love. This often happens to the children of addicts, in that one or both parents suffers from a blocked energy flow.

Sometimes an over-fed navel chakra in infancy can produce the same result as an underfed one. Parents who can only relate on the navel level due to their own blockages overstimulate the navel chakra of the child at the expense of the development of other centers. As the person grows to adulthood, navel over-emphasis can lead to addiction to food, drugs, or alcohol to reproduce the infantile oblivion. The person who is conditioned to relate predominantly on a navel level can suffer a feeling of isolation or not being loved when confronted with adults who relate through other chakras. The food or drug blots out the isolation.

It's easy to get hung up on a blockage. The only trouble is, it's not considered appropriate for an adult in our culture to be hung up on the navel area. Adults are supposed to be sexual, not dependent in the way of a child. The sexual chakra is conveniently located next door to the navel and is the energy outlet most readily accessible to it. Overemphasis on the navel area, then, is more acceptably translated as an overemphasis on sexuality—or on the kinds of power relationships between the sexes that can come from misuse of solar plexus energy, on the other side of the navel chakra. Both men and women can use sexuality as a disguised way of getting dependency needs met; promiscuity is often nothing more than intense neediness in disguise. The more oral the sexual expression, the more it may be serving navel purposes. Severe "Oedipal" problems are more related to the navel area than the sexual chakra.

Blocked Chakras, Sexuality, and Addiction

All chakras are created equal. The sexual chakra is only one of the centers, its expression no more and no less important to a balanced and healthy life than the expression of any other chakra. Yet, an outside observer of our culture might think it was the boss chakra from listening to the conversations, reading books, hearing our music, watching movies, and soaking up advertising. Why is there a disproportionate emphasis on the sexual chakra today? What we've just said about the navel chakra is one reason. There are others, related to what is happening in society.

Addictions, which most of us suffer in greater or lesser degree, dam up the heart chakra and progressively distort those below it. If your heart is frozen tight, your relationships suffer, and when your relationships suffer, your self-esteem (the solar plexus) is damaged. When your self-esteem is low, you reach for material goods, addictive substances, or dependent relationships to fill up the void. You may, by this time, have trouble releasing energy through the sexual chakra—or it may become the only energy outlet that IS functioning—so that sex gets a disproportionate amount of your attention.

This progression of energy distortion is true of the addict—but it's increasingly true of society as a whole. Part of the reason is that almost everybody has at least one or two addictions which affect their energy field—coffee, cigarettes, t.v., and on to addictions of greater severity. Other chemical pollutants also impinge on the free flow of energy.

The sexual chakra can be the source of addictive tendencies. The child who is stimulated to precocious sexuality by adults in the environment (or by the media) can divert excessive energy into that center which should go into a balanced and even development of all chakras. Traumatic events like molestation, incest, or rape can cause severe blockages so that the individual is deeply afraid of sexuality. Addiction can develop as a way of deadening the fear. Addiction in a parent can make sexual traumas more likely—for instance, some studies find that one incest victim in three has an alcoholic father. Essences which can help with sexual difficulties include BASIL, FIG, HIBISCUS, and STICKY MONKEYFLOWER.

How Man-Made Chemicals Compound the Chakra Problem

In our society we're constantly exposed to artificial substances—we breathe them, eat them, drink them, put them on our faces, and dye our hair with them. As suggested earlier, the human body has been exposed to organic substances for millions of years and is composed of similar substances, but this is not true with artificial chemicals. Thus, they can be extremely damaging. Manufactured drugs are far more damaging to those addicted to them than organic drugs are to those who are addicted to them.

Likewise, food additives, cosmetics, and industrial fumes can create damage to both the physical and subtle bodies in the long run.

Chemicals encountered in work, life, or diet can compound the damage done in the past and impede the healing work being attempted in the present. Additional cleansing may be needed if such chemicals have played a large part in your life. If your work or other circumstances make continued exposure to chemicals necessary, you may need to continue cleansing and protecting yourself to keep the healing going. Truck and taxi drivers, for instance, have a high rate of alcoholism, and this is partially due to the effects of constant bombardment of gasoline fumes on the liver.

The Importance of Chakra Repair in Healing Addictions

The chakras are crucial life force distributors which insure our ability to lead balanced and integrated lives, particularly in our relationships. Anything which goes wrong with the chakras can lead to imbalance and unhappiness. In the case of addictions, it's often hard to know which came first—chakra blockage or substance abuse. Sometimes early childhood traumas create chakra problems which later lead to addiction.

Nonetheless, the addictive substance itself does damage to the chakra system which must be repaired if the person is to lead a happy life. When the person simply stops the addiction but doesn't unblock the chakras, there's great danger that the pain of the isolation and of blocked energy flow will be so overwhelming that the person will revert to the addiction in order to deaden the pain. This is one reason why there are so many relapses that the addict and those who try to help become discouraged. The exercises which follow specifically help with unblocking and cleansing the chakras. Please know that the cleansing is a process, one you may have to repeat many times as new layers of healing are reached. Nonetheless, it's quite accessible to each of us, and the rewards are great in terms of more life energy and better relationships.

EXERCISE: Testing Your Chakras

This exercise is designed to be a diagnostic test of your chakras—their strength to give out and their strength to receive. Many of us do not think of it as a strength to be able to receive, but it takes a strong energy system to be able to absorb, a strong system to be able to take in love.

Sit quietly in a place where you won't be disturbed, and place yourself in such a way that you're facing a blank wall about five or six feet or so away. Create a bubble around yourself.

Imagine that at the place of each of your chakras there's a headlight, like on a car. Each of these lights can have a different color, or they can all be the same color, white or any you prefer at the time.

Working your way up from the bottom, one by one turn on all your lights and aim their beams at the opposite wall. Be aware of the relative strength of each of the beams. Notice which ones reach the wall, and which don't. See if you can find switches somewhere inside you that can turn up the weak ones and turn down the ones that are too strong.

Now imagine that the room you're sitting in is flooded with an incredible light. It may be white, blue, gold, or silver, and it's more powerful than any light you can imagine inside your body. This is the light of Spirit, and it's ever-present.

As you begin to see and to feel the light, notice that it's starting to surround your bubble, pass through the wall, and begin to fill it.
When your bubble is filled with the light, it will start to enter your chakras.

Notice which ones it can enter well, and which ones it has difficulty entering. Try to inhale and draw the light deeper and deeper into the chakras that it does not enter well. Notice that the chakras which don't give out well may not be the same as the chakras which don't receive well. For instance, you may be pouring out light from your third eye, but not taking any in.

When you have breathed in enough light to balance the chakras, rest in the light for a few moments, before you dissolve your bubble and return to the regular state of awareness.

Use this exercise regularly as a diagnostic tool, for measuring the strength of your energy, and for checking out the progress you're making in the work you're doing with yourself. This exercise will always tell you the state of your chakras when the mind is not sure.

Reopening the Heart Center—The Key to Healing Yourself

As important as the need for physical healing is the need for heart-healing. Without it, you may be sober/thin/drug-free, but still quite miserable. In order to feel happy, we need love, and, as long as the heart center remains closed, we can be in a happy crowd but still feel alone, cut off from our fellows. If we cleanse the heart, we don't have to worry so much about the mind. If the heart feels something, the mind will always get busy making up reasons why it should be so.

Many of the exercises in this book rely on the heart center as their healing locus, as it's such a key to restored health. First, however, there's a need to gently reopen that center, slowly, treating yourself lovingly, lest you should perceive that as pain.

There may, indeed, be some pain situated there, the pain of old losses, rejections, and hurts you've suffered. Heart-wounds are agonizing, of that there's no doubt, but a closed heart center keeps you from finding new people to love, from soaking up the love that is all around us all the time.

EXERCISE: The Many-Petalled Flower for the Heart Center

Place yourself in the bubble. Imagine your heart center as a beautiful many-petalled flower, with the petals facing outward and closed. A positive color for the flower would be bright pink, since that is the color of love. You may see it as a lotus, a rose, or as any many-petalled flower you may be drawn to.

Starting at the outside, allow the petals to open, one by one. With each petal, affirm your willingness to give and receive love. You may do it by saying inwardly, "I am open to love," or whatever seems pleasing to you. Actually moving your hands through your energy field as though you were opening the petals with them seems to increase the effect.

Keep opening petals and opening petals and opening petals, repeating the affirmations as you do.

As you near the center, notice that the petals are glowing with pink light, warm to the touch.

When the center itself is open, the pink light radiates from it and pulsates outward past the edge of your bubble. You say to yourself, "This light from my heart is a beacon to those who would rightfully share love with me." Draw down pink light energy from your Core Self and let it pour outward.

Now rotate the flower so it turns inward, and slowly let your entire body fill with pink light. It's so easy to become dependent on other people for the love we need, but we all have the power to connect with universal love energy directly and become filled with it. Say to yourself, "I am loving and filled with love."

To close the exercise, rotate your flower so it's facing outward again, and close the petals of the flower. Many of us can open the flower well, but don't know how to close it and end up being involved too quickly, with highly inappropriate people. Knowing how to close the heart flower is just as important as knowing how to open it. Then it opens when we want it to, not when we're addicted to having it open.

Repeat this exercise for a few days. It's a nice one to do before you go to sleep, because it's soothing and because the heart-healing will continue in your dreams. How will you know when your heart center is open? There's no mistaking it. You will have brand new sensations in the area of your physical heart—electrical currents of energy flowing in and out. When someone shows up whom you care for, there may be a leap in that area, a sudden, short pulsing not unlike a small orgasm. You will suddenly know what certain phrases in the language mean, phrases like "My heart went out to her," "My heart jumped for joy," and, alas, what heartache truly is. You'll also know why all those gooey love songs harp on the heart.

The newly-opened heart center is fearful and readily closes its petals down again at so much as a cross word. At first, you need to keep reopening it, but is the exercise not a pleasant one, literally a labor of love? Doing it will start you on the path of emotional and spiritual healing and to filling your life with the fellowship of loving friends and mates.

When you begin to open this center, you may at first experience some pain. There are heart wounds, certainly, that need healing. Let yourself cry over those things, because tears are the best known cleansing agent for the heart. The pain is broken down, dissolved, and released by the tears. No matter if it happened 20 years ago, if there's still pain, you need to cry, but do it within a transmuting bubble of white light.

Another reason the heart center opening is sometimes experienced as painful is that the energy body of an addict is so used to being closed down tight that when you begin to open it, you may hold on with all your might. You may reassure yourself by massaging the chest area, but it would be even more reassuring to have a loving person do it, particularly one who has already been through the opening process. The person doing the massage should consciously direct into their hands a flow of love and pink light.

Since the heart center is powerfully affected by sugar and alcohol, the essence BLEEDING HEART would be important for all those with sugar or alcohol problems, for it helps repair the heart chakra from major wounds and losses. The healing crisis with this remedy can be difficult if buried grief comes to the surface, so always check with a pendulum or muscle reflexes to see if you're up to it. Where grief is the issue, the essence EUCALYPTUS is quite healing. The gem essences ROSE

QUARTZ, TURQUOISE, AND RUBY are all good for the heart center and are more gentle than some of the other gem essences.

As for stones themselves, wearing or having rose quartz near you would also be very healing, since that is the heart center stone. Perhaps you can get a necklace of rose quartz beads, just long enough to cover the heart. Pink tourmaline and pink kunzite are also good for healing and opening the heart.

Techniques for Cleansing the Chakras

Other than the heart, it's usually best to open all of the chakras together, rather than focus on a single center, so you don't create an imbalance. If you opened the brow and crown centers for psychic and spiritual work without cleansing and opening the centers below it, you could open yourself to some rather unbalanced sensations and experiences. Opening the sexual chakra without attention to the heart and head could lead to heartless and distorted relationships. Thus it's best to attend to all of them equally.

EXERCISE: The Whirlpool Cleanse for Chakras

Envision the chakras and locate them within your body, as in the diagram given earlier.

Erect the bubble and fill it with a particular color of light, according to your intuition. For many purposes, white light is best, as it contains all the other colors.

Begin with the root chakra. Create a whirlpool or funnel of light that is pointing at the chakra. Let this whirlpool swirl into the chakra like a tornado, spinning and sucking out any dark areas or obstructions that prevent you from feeling grounded. The light will keep on spinning for as long as it needs to, even though you move on to other centers.

Go on to the sexual chakra and erect another whirlpool, which again blazes up and consumes obstacles. Here the difficulty to be healed would be in a balanced and healthy outflowing of sexual energy.

When the areas below feel relatively clear, move on to the solar plexus and start a whirlpool there. In this area, the light would blaze up and burn away obstructions to a healthy, realistic self-esteem, dissolving old ego wounds and feelings of lack of confidence.

Letting the previous whirlpools continue to spin, move on to the heart center and start one there. The heart center, being so crucial and vulnerable, can stand any amount of cleansing, as older and deeper heart wounds surface to be dealt with. Here the light would burn obstructions to loving and being loved.

Now move on to the thymus chakra. This one will probably not feel blocked, but simply unopened. Use the whirlpool here to help you awaken this new center. Feel yourself connected to the world in a peaceful, nurturing way.

Next, erect a whirlpool at the throat center, where it would burn away obstructions to communication and also to a free flow of money.

Next, do the brow center, which would relieve obstacles to the creative and psychic energy flow.

Finally, make a whirlpool at the crown, which would cleanse obstacles to meditation and inspiration and open up your spiritual connection with all that is.

Observe which of the centers still have whirlpools spinning, as these may need special work. Blaze up the light brightly in those areas for a few moments before stopping them all and dissolving the bubble.

Repeat this over a few days until the chakras seem clear. Later, repeat with different colors as your intuition guides you. Even when you've finished, repeat the cleansing process periodically to avoid the buildup of new obstructions in the course of daily living or from your minor addictions.

EXERCISE: A Bouquet of Chakra Flowers

If you've done the foregoing cleansing to completion, it may be safe for you to focus on a particular flower especially relevant to your own personal needs. Nonetheless, over a period of time, you should take care to cultivate the whole garden rather than a single flower. A single, perfect rose is nice if your resources are limited, but in our vision we can afford a whole bouquet. Each of the centers may have a different color and type of flower, but yours may be different than other people's. For some, these colors move up the spectrum of the rainbow, starting with red at the root chakra.

Sit in your bubble. Tune into your chakras and feel that each of them is a flower about to bud. Feel that all these flowers are facing outward, away from your body.

Slowly, a petal at a time, starting at your root chakra, feel that each of these flowers begins to open. You may want to place your hands over each chakra, and repeat an affirmation. For instance, for the root chakra, I AM ROOTED IN MY BODY AND MY LIFE; for the sexual chakra, I AM OPEN TO MY SEXUALITY AND MY CREATIVITY; for the solar plexus, I AM STRONG AND CLEAR AND IN CHARGE OF MY LIFE; for the heart center, I AM LOVING AND NURTURING; and so on. Design ones which specifically relate to your own personal needs.

Notice that as the center of the flower reveals itself, there is a warm light in there that shines outward, illuminating your bubble and shining out into the world.

When the process feels complete, keep the flowers with you, but dissolve the bubble.

If you do this several times for each of the chakras, you'll begin to feel a quickening of energies in those areas. The flowers may need to be reopened from time to time, since they readily close down with stress, fatigue, rough experiences, or overdoing it on some of your minor addictions. You can also imagine flowers opening in any body organ that is actually or symbolically deadened by the addiction. For instance, you could visualize flowers opening in the ears if you felt the need to be a better listener or in the eyes if you wanted a deeper appreciation of art.

If you're the sort who gives freely to others but has difficulty receiving, imagine that there are closed flowers facing the interior of the body at each of the chakra points. Opening them repeatedly with an affirmation such as "I am willing to receive," will help balance the energy flow. When the energy only goes outward and you take nothing in, you ultimately feel depleted and resentful, and you're tempted to abuse some substance in order to fill the resulting emptiness.

EXERCISE: Plastering the Cracks in Your Chakras

As your intuitive capacities stretch out and unfold in the course of doing this work, you may come to sense that there are actual breaks in some of your chakras. Traumas and tragedies are especially prone to cause such breaks, and sometimes the addiction develops as a way of stopping up the hole or filling the void with which such damage leaves you.

There's no statute of limitations on chakra ruptures—if sufficiently devastating, they can be inherited. The parent with a chakra insufficiency hasn't the ability to nurture that chakra fully in the child. When one of our recovering clients, a sugar addict, went to Ireland, she intuitively discovered that the root chakra rupture caused by her great-great grandfather's emigration to America when his family was wiped out in the potato famine had been passed down to all the succeeding generations. That side of the family had been affected by sugar and alcohol addiction in each succeeding generation and was also unable to establish roots anywhere, moving frequently.

She was the first family member to go to Ireland since the emigration, and found it incredibly moving. There on the docks in County Cork, where the great-great grandfather had gotten on the boat, she used the exercise which follows to repair her root chakra. She also went through the same exercise on behalf of each member of the family she knew about, living and dead, in all the generations since, down to the newborn baby of her niece.

Here are the steps:

Identify a chakra which needs repair, using your intuition or the exercise on testing your chakra.

Go into a deeper state of consciousness, and call on your Core Self for help in repairing this center.

Imagine that you're shrinking until you're small enough to fit into the chakra.

Now enter the chakra, and sense it as a small but cozy room that surrounds you, something like an egg. Fill it with light in the color of your choice, perhaps blue, since a broken chakra is likely to be full of fear.

Scan the walls of the chakra with your mind, and locate the breaks.

Imagine that you're using a liquid light to fill up the breaks.

Use light-liquid to paint the walls of the whole room.

Leave the room, and return to your normal size.

EXERCISE: Filling and Feeding Your Chakras

The feeling of being drained by others or drained of strength to work on your life is a strong pull back into your old addictions or into creating new ones, like eating too much. Even when the chakras are clean and clear, you may still need to know how to pull in more energy from your Core Self and spiritual sources.

Get into a bubble of a color you're inspired to choose. Go down deeply into a state of meditation.
Make a strong link with your Core Self. It may help to envision it as a cord of light going from you upwards.

Tell your Core Self you need strength and energy to complete your tasks.

Imagine energy traveling down the cord into your various centers. If there's one center that especially needs energizing and strengthening, imagine the cord attached there.

When you sense that enough new energy has come in, dissolve the cord, the link, and the bubble.

Please note that this exercise is no substitute for rest. It's not to be used to help you churn out work without the needed periods of play. In some of us, workaholism is the primary addiction, and substance abuse only secondary, as a means of continuing the workaholism or unwinding from it.

EXERCISE: For Linking the Energy of Your Chakras

Our chakras do not function in isolation from each other. The same energy flows through all of them, linking them, weaving them together. Our chakras are linked from root to crown, in a vertical column that loops around the body connecting them all. As it pours out of each chakra, the energy is shaped by that chakra, rather like dough being put through a pasta machine. It's the same dough, but if you change the openings you can get thick or thin spaghetti, ziti, shells, wagon wheels. So the energy is the same, but its shape, its manifestation, changes.

Sometimes we're damaged in a certain chakra and another stronger one can lend energy to strengthen it. And as we will see later in the book, different addictive substances affect, activate, and damage different chakras. Certain specific substances as well are abused in the effort to link certain of the chakras together. In this exercise you'll be learning to link together the energy of your different chakras, to heal them and to use them together in the patterns you're accustomed to using with your favorite drugs.

Sit quietly and feel your breathing. One by one, become aware of all your chakras as you did in an earlier exercise.

Begin by focusing on your root chakra. Feel that a strand of energy, or light, emerges from the back of your root chakra and moves up your back toward your sexual chakra. Feel the energy connect with that chakra, and then emerge from the front of it, circling down the front of your body until it meets your root chakra again.

Now feel that there's a continuous circle of energy moving between these two chakras, linking and balancing them. You've gotten to know the chakras individually. How does it feel to have two turned on together? Is this energy familiar and comfortable?

Dissolve the connection between those two chakras, but keep your focus on your root chakra. Now create an energy loop that goes up your back from your root chakra to your solar plexus chakra, then down the front to the root chakra again. Notice how it feels, and the ways that this connection feels different than the root/sexual chakra linkage.

Slowly, starting each time with your root chakra, move up your body and link it to your heart, thymus, throat, brow, and crown chakras. Notice each time how it feels, and the ways in which it feels different than the other connections. Pay attention to the combinations that are strong and the ones that are weak, which are easier to do and which are harder.

When you've gone through all the chakras once, go back to your root and sexual chakras and turn them on like headlights so they're shining out from your body. Feel that their beams merge into one unified ray in front of you.

One-by-one go through the pairs of chakras—root and solar plexus, root and heart, and root and thymus—turning on the beams and shining them out so that they merge into one light (as you did with the root and sexual chakras.) Ask yourself the same questions about feeling, strength, blockage, and so on.

When you've gone through all the connections, and balanced them as much as you can for now, sit quietly in your bubble for a while and feel that there's an internal circuit that connects all these chakras. It travels up the back of your body and down the front. Feel the energy circulating and feel all your chakras shine.

Now slowly turn off all the lights and dissolve your bubble.

EXERCISE: Second Part

When you've done the above exercise a number of times and feel the chakra linkage proceding smoothly, here is a further development.

On separate days, moving up the body, work on connecting the sexual chakra to all the other chakras. Then connect the solar plexus to all the other chakras, and then do the same to the heart and the higher chakras. When you've gone through this exercise eight times, starting with each of the main chakras and connecting it with all the others, you're ready to start playing. Make up any combination you like. Connect root to crown, sexual to brow, thymus to root, or solar plexus to heart. Let yourself dance among all the chakras.

If any of them seem particularly weak, you might want to try hooking them up with a chakra that seems strong to see if it can lend it energy to balance it out. When you get to the chapters on individual addictions, you'll want to come back to this exercise and work with chakras that may have been damaged due to your particular addictions.

Repairing Chakra Damage with Essences and Stones

In the first book, we discussed the essences and stones and how they can help with addictive patterns. These power tools act on the subtle bodies most strongly, and thus a number are excellent at repairing the damage addictions do to subtle bodies and the chakras. Exercises given here have helped you determine which of your own chakras could have been most damaged. The two charts printed here show the chakras, which addictions most affect them, and which stones, remedies, and other tools help repair or strengthen them.

Not all of the essences listed are described in this book, because not all of them are used in Donna's work. In choosing which ones to use, it would be helpful to read the complete description of each remedy in Gurudas' book, *Flower Essences And Vibrational Healing*, (See bibliography for essences in the Appendix.) In addition, you may want to test with a pendulum which of the remedies listed under a given chakra are best for you, as well as which chakra you should work with at this time. Stones are also suggested which strengthen each of the chakras. Different books on the subject list different stones, but these are the main ones.

The Chakras, Addictions, And Remedies To Repair Them

CHAKRAS	ADDICTIONS	STONES	REMEDIES TO HELP IN AFFECTING IT, HELPING IT, REPAIRING IT
ROOT	COFFEE MARIJUANA HEROIN	SMOKEY QUARTZ GARNET, ONYX TOURMALINE	COMFREY, LOOSESTRIFE, ROOT SQUASH, CORN, CLEMATIS STAR OF BETHLEHEM
SEXUAL	SUGAR, ALCOHOL AMPHETAMINE COCAINE	RUBY, AMBER CARNELIAN CITRINE	LOOSESTRIFE, POMEGRANATE, SQUASH, WATERMELON HIBISCUS, IRIS, FIG
SOLAR PLEXUS	COFFEE CIGARETTES HEROIN	GR. TOURMALINE PERIDOT MALACHITE	AMARANTHUS, AVOCADO BLOODROOT, CENTURY AGAVE, COSMOS, SUNFLOWER, MANGO, HYSSOP, PENNYROYAL, SAGE
HEART	ALCOHOL SUGAR	ROSE QUARTZ PINK TOURMALINE RHODOCHROSITE	ALOE VERA, AMANTHUS BLEEDING HEART, BORAGE, COSMOS HELLBORUS, PAPAYA
THYMUS	MARIJUANA SYNTHETIC DRUGS	MALACHITE EMERALD RODOCHROSITE	ALMOND, AMARANTHUS,THYMUS BLEEDING HEART, EUCALYPTUS MARIGOLD, DAFFODIL
THROAT	CIGARETTES MARIJUANA	TURQUOISE AQUAMARINE CHRYSOCOLLA	ALMOND, CALIFORNIA POPPY CELANDINE, COSMOS, FIG MANGO, PASSION FLOWER
BROW	COFFEE, COCAINE CIGARETTES MARIJUANA	AMETHYST LAPIS FLOURITE	AMARANTHUS, CHAMOMILE MANGO, NASTURTIUM, DILL HOPS, REDWOOD, GREEN ROSE
CROWN	SYNTHETIC DRUGS COCAINE MARIJUANA	CLEAR QUARTZ DIAMOND	AMANTHUS, SKULLCAP FORGET ME NOT, LOTUS ROSEMARY, LAVENDER, DILL
ALL	MASSIVE LONG TERM SYNTHETIC DRUGS	CLEAR QUARTZ AMETHYST	ANGELICA, CHAPPARAL LOTUS, LOOSESTRIFE SHOOTING STAR, LILAC

The Chakras And Additional Tools To Repair Them

CHAKRA	MUSICAL NOTE	COLORS	SPICES & HERBS	ART FORM RELATED TO THIS CHAKRA
ROOT	C	RED	GINGER, CHICORY, GINSENG	CRAFTS, THE HOUSEHOLD ARTS
SEXUAL	D	ORANGE	POPPY, SESAME, CARAWAY	DANCE
SOLAR PLEXUS	E	YELLOW	GARLIC, ONION	ACTING
HEART	F	GREEN (PINK)	CHAMOMILE, DANDELION	THE HEALING ARTS
THYMUS	G F#	BLUE-GREEN	CLOVES, ANIS, FENNEL	
THROAT	G A	BLUE	CHILI, CURRY, CINNAMON	MUSIC
BROW	A B	PURPLE INDIGO LAVENDER	EUCAPLYTUS WINTERGREEN	WRITING, PAINTING
CROWN	B High C	PURPLE WHITE, GOLD	DILL, YARROW, PARSLEY	PSYCHIC GIFTS, CHANNELING

CHAPTER TWO

THE KARMA OF ADDICTONS: PATTERNS IN PAST LIVES

An Introduction to Reincarnation

As one way of understanding the WHYS of addiction, we looked into the part played by past lives of the addicts, with whom we worked. To briefly review the basic ideas about reincarnation: There is a common belief among spiritual seekers around the world that we are immortal and that we have lived many times, in many eras and places, in different bodies, as different personalities. The stories of these lives are supposedly available to us through meditation, dreams, hypnotic regression, or through the services of a psychic like co-author Andrew, who has this ability.

Psychic researchers over the past century have investigated and documented many cases suggestive of reincarnation, such as memories by small children of another recent life, which then checked out in detail. (The classic work in this area is Ian Stevenson's *Twenty Cases Suggestive Of Reincarnation*.) The most modern and scientific of these investigations was by psychologist Helen Wambaugh, who hypnotized hundreds of ordinary people, most of whom did not have any special knowledge or belief in reincarnation. She was able to uncover past life memories in the great majority of her subjects, as well as knowledge of that before-birth state we have been discussing, wherein the life task, purpose, parents, and special experiences are all planned in advance. If you would like to know about the principles of rebirth she uncovered, you might enjoy her book, *Life Before Life*, published by Bantam in 1979. (Other books on the subject of reincarnation are listed in the bibliography in the Appendix.)

One theory about the purpose of reincarnation is that it provides the soul with all the experiences of what it means to be human in different times, places, and life circumstances. As we shall see, one life experience which every soul chooses to go through in one or several lifetimes is addiction. In many cases, as the past life readings given later will show, addiction is not running from the vision, but is a part of the vision, a part of the planned life experience to make up the total personality you become. For instance, it may be a choice in order to better help other addicts, since many who recover from their addictions then go on to become the most effective healers of other addicted people.

The process of learning about past lives can be very healing for the addicted person. People who think they only have one shot at life and who inexplicably spend most of their life in the maelstrom of addiction can feel a great deal of self-hate. Coming to understand the longer-range function of the addiction as well as the truth of our immortality can be a great relief. Also, we can put an end to the sense of isolation addiction locks us into when we experience ourselves as male, female, straight, gay, black, white, yellow, red, rich, poor, deaf, blind, or otherwise handicapped. There arises a sense of oneness with the human community which eliminates our inner sense of fragmentation.

Several of the addicts who worked with us went for past life readings with Andrew. They will share their readings with you later. They found this knowledge helpful in their recovery, enabling them to make sense of certain situations and tendencies in the present. Nonetheless, it is not important, for the purposes of this book, whether you believe in reincarnation or not. We'll be giving you a process for uncovering past life memories, but you who have difficulty accepting the concept may use the stories the same way you would use a dream in Gestalt therapy, acting out the story or retelling it so you become every character yourself. Each character reflects an aspect of you. Similarly, a dream occurs in the privacy of your brain, and even though you may dream about your mother or father, in the dream they represent parts of yourself.

In much the same way, in reincarnational memories or readings, the "selves" uncovered are also aspects of your total self. They're inner counterparts to our biological relatives.We're affected by them in much the same sense we're affected by the life experiences of our physical relatives—saddened when they're sad, happy when they're happy, frightened when they're frightened. So, too, on a more subtle level, we're influenced by the life experiences of our incarnational relatives. Whether we believe these selves are real or see them only as externalized reflections of aspects of our psyche, they're nonetheless useful to study.

You may regard them as possibilities or potentialities latent within yourself, ways that you might function under a variety of circumstances. They're the roads not taken but still beckoning, and if you study those roads through the story fragments, you will learn a great deal about yourself. Just as a drama enacted in a dream has no presence in waking reality yet can be a way of learning some lesson, the reincarnational histories can be a way of learning without the necessity of direct experience. Consider them tools for learning, without struggling over their reality or lack of it. A novel or a poem may be entirely fictional yet have a healing impact on the reality of each reader. Likewise, if an experience related to reincarnation has a strong emotional impact, then it has validity, whether or not it's "real" in any scientifically-proveable way.

Karma Shmarma

No treatment of the subject of reincarnation is complete without considering KARMA—the notion that actions and conditions in one lifetime can have an influence on subsequent lives. In this scheme of things, for instance, to have ridiculed and badly mistreated a drunken mother in one life may mean having to be a drunk yourself in another life. Or, to have robbed people in this life to pay for your drugs may mean that you must yourself be robbed repeatedly in this life or the next. Whether or not the more difficult memories about past lives uncovered by the exercises we'll give you are true—and how can one prove or disprove them?—the point once more is how you use what you have uncovered. Do you use this belief system to make yourself a better person or do you use it to make yourself more miserable?

The typical addict is full of self-hate and can use the teachings about reincarnation and karma to heap on even greater loads of guilt and self-loathing. If you attribute your addiction and other kinds of suffering to punishment for misdeeds in previous lives, then it's even harder to let go of it, because you feel you must deserve it. If you believe that mistakes made in the course of your addiction doom you to terrible retribution in later years or in some future incarnation, then your guilt and fear are overwhelming, and you may want to drink/drug/eat to blot out your fear of the future.

Another way the self-hate of the addict can distort the process of working with past lives is in the common mistake of believing that you were someone very famous or rich in a past life, and then focusing on this past glory to feel good about yourself again. There was only one Marie Antoinette, only one Cleopatra, only one Napoleon, and yet there are an abundance of people who claim to have been these entities. Even in these relatively affluent times, the vast majority of lives on the planet are lived in poverty. There were ever more slaves and serfs than masters and kings. If the only lives you uncover are those of wealth and glory, doubt your information. If you remember being Marie Antoinette, perhaps you have the correct era, perhaps you were even in her court, but you're far more likely to have been her servant than Marie herself. You could be remembering the circumstances, but blotting out the inglorious details.

However, if you've remembered lives in which you did wrong, take it easy on yourself. The point is, karma is not about punishment, it's an educational tool. The only desire the Highest has for us is that we constantly grow in love and wisdom. In that before-life period, we selected both our life task and certain experiences as tools for growth. In the section which follows, we'll see that you may have selected your addiction as just such a tool for growth. It wasn't necessarily a fall from grace, but quite possibly a deliberate and even necessary choice.

Some of the experiences you chose may have been quite painful, yet they, too, were chosen as a way of growing, not for the sake of punishment or "bad karma." Just as athletes sometime suffer pain in training to increase their physical capacities, so, too, do painful experiences, if used correctly increase our strength and capacities on the emotional and spiritual levels. The athlete does not regard the sore muscles as punishment; neither should you regard your emotional pain in that way.

In the course of many incarnations, the greater being you are only a small part of—the being we're calling your Core Self—desires to experience life from every conceivable point of view. Thus, in some lives it will be the master and in others the slave; in some lives the killer and in others the murder victim; in some lives the prostitute and in others the celibate priest. In some lifetimes, inevitably, it will be the addict, while in others it will be the child at the mercy of the addicted parent. The scales tend to balance over thousands of years, and it is the balancing of the scales which those on the spiritual path call karma. In this eternal series of experiences, nothing we do is "bad" because sooner or later something will be learned from it which carries the Core Self closer to perfection. However, we do not only learn from suffering, though some of us learn best that way, or there would be no need for so much of it. We can learn from expanding our consciousness, from deliberate attention to understanding and mastering our emotions, from all those self-improvement efforts. Most of all, we can grow through reuniting with the spiritual dimensions of reality, especially by tapping into the greater wisdom, strength and love of the Core Self.

What, then if you feel you harmed others by acts of omission or commission in the course of your addiction or in a past life—will you uncover? Will you have to be on the receiving end of these same hurtful actions as a way of balancing the scales? Nothing is as simple as it seems. You may have entered into an agreement before birth with that person to do that particular thing as a way of helping them grow. How do you know the end result was harmful? For instance, in the long run, the child of an alcoholic mother may develop a wonderful creative talent by living in a dream world to escape the chaos. The child may have selected the parent for just that very reason. There's no way of knowing the purpose of any given circumstance. We're incredibly myopic, and we cannot know the meaning of any experience, because that depends on what the person ultimately makes of it.

Nonetheless, there are, doubtless things you did in the course of your addiction for which you're sorry. Guilt is the most corrosive of emotions, the most harmful to your self-esteem. There are processes within the Twelve Steps of A.A. that help to offset karma and help cleanse you of guilt. (Steps Eight and Nine are described fully in the A. A. book, *The Twelve Steps And Twelve Traditions*, available at A.A. meetings which are open to the public, or at the public library.) Remedies and exercises for cleansing guilt are also given in the first book of this series on treating addictions.

The Karma of Addictions

Everyone is addicted at some point in their reincarnational history. That's one thing everyone who incarnates here has to go through. As important as it is to experience wholeness, we also have to experience the destruction and disintegration of wholeness. Addictions are one way of breaking down the center of wholeness. Madness is another.

The positive side of the process of addiction is the paradoxical realization that we continue to be human even when we are no longer centered. Often it's the process of being an addict that gets us to realize the immortality of the Core Self. As we destroy everything we care about and as we destroy the body, we come to the consciousness that something still exists. There's always something out there that's timeless, and it isn't the personality self.

Often great sages have been alcoholics or drug addicts in their immediately preceding past lives. Often great creative artists are addicts beginning to capture the vision because they've opened up that place on some level. When you destroy your body, your relationships with everyone, and your personality, you're taking a step toward liberating the true self, the spirit. Addiction is a negative way of doing that, but it is one way. It's not very different from Zen, if you look at it on that level. You alienate your spouse, children, and siblings. You vaguely remember that once you weren't this way, but it's hard to get back to. Everything that human beings do is a tool for furthering consciousness, no matter how hideously cruel. Everything is a tool. Even abdication of consciousness is a tool for furthering consciousness. If people who are abandoning consciousness would recognize it as a tool for enhancing consciousness, if they knew that they cannot run away, then they might stop trying.

A pattern which deserves mentioning is the karma of slavery. The derivation of the word addict has specifically to do with slavery. One of the roles each of us takes on, possibly repeatedly in the course of many lifetimes, is that of slave. Since the world is now at a point in evolution when overt slavery has been eliminated, those who are working their way out of the slave mode of behavior seek another way of remaining a slave. Many of the negative traits attributed to the addictive personality—the deceptiveness, the ingratiation, the hiding, even the defiance—have more to do with character patterns established during chains of lives in slavery than with the addiction itself.

In addiction, you're enslaved to the power tool, yet it's an upgrading in the process, because in real slavery the slave and master were two different people. When you're addicted, the slave and master are the same. It's an evolutionary step close to resolution of the pattern of limitations many of us are working out.

Another pattern common now is with people who died in recent wars and came back quickly. Where they were drugged or drunk at death—for example, those who were using morphine as a pain killer and became addicted—the attraction to the drug may carry on into this life. Many of the young people who are dying of drugs or drinking are doing it to clear out that wartime death. Likewise, those who do a lot of drugs or alcohol in high school and college and then are able to stop have worked it through. The ages in your current life when important things happen to you often mirror crucial ages in past lives, so the ages from 18 to 21 are important for many who died as young soldiers. Where that wartime death was part of an addictive chain of lives, however, it's harder to work through. As one additional variation—though not at all a common one—some people who poisoned others are working out their karma by poisoning themselves with alcohol or drugs.

Addictions as Intercultural Incarnation Bridges

We're also going to find that incarnational histories have a relationship to the type of substance you are drawn to. We change only gradually from incarnation to incarnation, and a big change in cultural rootedness requires a major adjustment. Sometimes an addiction serves as a bridge in such circumstances. As you'll read in the chapter on tobacco, many heavy smokers are former Native Americans—as are those drawn to other natural consciousness-altering substances.

Heroin abusers are often those with a history of many oriental lives who are now switching over into western incarnation. They are doing this in masses—as are many with western histories being born into the east— to further the aim of integrating East and West into one planetary civilization. The 1940-1950s era of massive numbers of deaths due to war followed by a baby boom provided the opportunity for large numbers to make this shift. For those with a long eastern history, however, heroin reminds them of the opium with which they were more familiar in their own cultures. Heroin serves to obliterate the homesickness and the sense of a drastic uprooting.

Epidemiologists who study the origins of disease have found that alcohol abuse is high among the first and second generations of certain national origins who immigrated into the United States, even though alcohol is not a major problem in their own country. Alcohol has a strong effect on the heart chakra, and here the issue is all the loved ones left behind, still incarnating in the other culture. We will find, however, that the problem does not stop at the second generation, but continues, as it has with black people and others who've been in this country for numbers of generations.

Past Life Readings for Some Recovering Addicts

The past life readings which follow were done for individuals who are recovering from their addictions and are used here with their permission. They illustrate a number of patterns and themes common to addictive lifetimes. You will note that often there is a chain of such lifetimes, rather than just a single one, and that the person has made the deliberate choice of the addiction as a means of exploring or working through a particular issue.

SUBJECT ONE: MILLIE

Millie is a 24-year-old woman with a history of multiple addictions in her teens, which ended when she went to A.A. at 19. Andrew begins by channeling her immediate past life, in a poor but educated radical working class family in Paris in the period before World War I.

"You had a brother seven years older who was a poet, and there was an enormous rivalry between you. There was an atmosphere of decadence which everyone was into, but you got into it heavily as a way of surpassing your brother. If he got drunk, you had to get drunker; if he went to two whore houses, you went to six; if he did cocaine, you did opium—whatever it was, you had to outdo him."

"He had a cruel streak and liked to see you suffer. He enjoyed the power he had to make you do these things. He resented your birth, since he was a mama's boy for seven years until you were born and then you became the favorite. His way of getting revenge on your mother was by ruining you. He also felt he was a scientific poet, working in the laboratory of human emotions, and that his experimenting on you was therefore justified."

"One of the reasons you came back without siblings in this life was as a way of getting out of that pattern. But there was this whole circle around your brother, and some of the people from that group may appear in this life. There are patterns you still have of locking into people which arise from that time. In that group, the highest state of life was to be drunk and pass out; it was so romanticized that in order to belong you had little choice. In that life, just as in this one, you had an alcoholic father who died when you were quite young, so the pattern is there, but the most important factor is that game between you and your brother."

"People seem to have different patterns about addiction. Yours seems to be very short—only two lifetimes—and it seems like it would be easy to get out of. The other lifetime in the pattern is in Spain in the early 1800's. Your mother was Spanish and your father a German diplomat, you being the product of a brief affair in which he seduced and left her. She spent the rest of her life going to church and repenting, as her guilt made her religiously devout.

"You had some kind of degenerative bone disease, so you were crippled and your legs were very weak. You were always in pain, and there weren't any pain killers, so you drank out of necessity, to stop the pain. Thus you were dependent on alcohol, yet not in the way you were in your current lifetime. It was medicinal, not for pleasure. Your body was so damaged, and you were in such intense pain that your body would leech the alcohol out of your system and use it like aspirin. You never got drunk, because it took so much alcohol to kill the pain.

"You also drank out of anger and lack of faith in a God who would put you in such a position—the pain, the inability to lead a normal life, the mysterious father, the lies and dishonesty your family put out about your birth. You kept going through crises of faith. You were also angry at your mother for getting you in this mess.

"You felt terribly isolated and different, an only child in an enormous family of relatives and cousins. You were shut away from the world and increasingly developed a yearning for a big brother who would go out in the world and bring it to you. This yearning was one of the main reasons you were attracted to the family in Paris in the next lifetime. All you saw was that the brother would be worldly and surrounded by people; you didn't see his ruinous cruelty. So in Paris you were sucked into a life of almost the opposite extreme, of total immersion in people, yet of the debauchery that ruined you. In this life, you are seeking a balance."

MILLIE: "I used to be incredibly fascinated by decadence, like the parts of the counter-culture that revered drugs. The songs I write are often about decadence, drugs, or prostitution. But I still keep a balance with it and don't get swallowed up by it."

ANDREW: "Yes, it's the balance that you're still striving to achieve. Even though in your current life you went into addictions massively and self-destructively, there was somehow a detachment from them. Because there was so much loneliness involved that you never got the sense of belonging you sought, you gained a distance from it that helped you get out.

"In your case, because the past life pattern is such a short one, it should be easier to heal, even though you went into it so heavily. It's like the difference between trying to recuperate from a week of really bad pneumonia as opposed to four months of really bad pneumonia. It's easier, even though it's very intense. People who have many lives around addictions get used to it, like living in a war zone. But for you, the memory that life wasn't always like that is shocking; it gives the addiction strength and intensity. But since it's a short pattern, it's also easier to get out of. The key, however, is in using the knowledge, the way you use it in the songs you write. You may—and should—keep on using music as a way of processing the information, even if you're 80 years old and haven't had a drink in 57 years, but you're still writing songs about alcoholics. Not only will they help keep you free of addictions, but they will also help those who listen to them."

SUBJECT TWO: NORA

Nora, to whom this book is dedicated, is a thirty year old woman who drank alcoholically for ten years and periodically abused pills. She has been sober several years now through A.A. Her mother is an alcoholic who sobered up on her own some years ago because the drinking was about to kill her. Her father is a heavy daily drinker who uses alcohol as a crutch to make it through life, as does her younger brother. Her sister is a compulsive overeater with periodic addiction to diet pills. She has many alcoholic relatives.

ANDREW: "What's coming up here is a pattern that is apparently common to your family's alcoholism and to a great many people. There are whole reincarnational communities, groups of people who often reincarnate together. Yours is made up of people who've spent many lifetimes being close to the earth and often working with the earth. All the people in your family have been connected in chains of lifetimes, working the land, and often making wine. A problem arises when that tie is broken by the move to industrial cities and the immigration to this country.

"There are psychic tribes of people who work together on certain tasks, who move in and out of different experiences together. There are probably several hundred in each tribe, but they're not all alive at once. I feel that you're part of a large tribe which has made a recent collective choice to explore alienation, and an easy way to be alienated is to have an addiction.

"After all those lifetimes of grounding, your group in the current life is ready to move out. Alienation is a tool for letting go of the grounding. The first step is to let go of being physically rooted, becoming like a pilgrim. From that you can move beyond grounding, so you can either not come back home or only come back as a visitor, in a totally different capacity.

"Another way to experience alienation is to be part of a family that cannot relate to one another, and yours was like that. Despite all the pain, the upshot of the life experience is to learn about alienation. It's like when you're watching a tragic movie, and you cry, and everyone dies in the end, but when it's all over, you realize it was just a movie, and the real you is still there. Because of your own long chain of lifetimes working the land, you're incredibly grounded, in a way that some of your family members are not.

"The collectives aren't together in all lifetimes. Members can go off on research excursions for a lifetime or two by themselves. The last time your collective was together was in northern Italy in the time of Napolean. All of you were villagers steeped in an old, old way of life that was being threatened by the upheavals of that Napoleanic era of conquest and rebellion. The collective made the choice to stay very grounded, so the upheaval wouldn't affect them so much. The choice the group has made in this current life is to experiment with fragmentation by drifting and not being connected. Very often what happens when you do that is you get a little lost as individuals, particularly because the group isn't used to fragmentation. This culture supports individuals getting lost. What you're trying to achieve is being grounded inside without being grounded outside by the earth. Now the tribe isn't going to be born in the same place, so the tendency to get lost is stronger. Some members of your group are totally lost now, and some are doing well.

"You personally have lost the inner grounding a little more than you need or want to. You've made the choice not to be grounded by a place, but you've left some of the grounding behind you, and you need to go back and get it. There were important discoveries you made as a child about the world and people, and a sense of joy that you've lost track of and need to go back and reclaim. Once you recapture that joy, it will change the nature of any kind of addiction.

"Once you recapture it, through various kinds of healing work, you're going to act as a catalyst for others in your group. You'll remind them that you all came here to do something, and you've all been lost and goofing off. The reminding won't be in words, but on a deeper level. The changes you make in your energy field will affect many of the people around you— the alcoholics in your A.A. group, for example. It will open up their windows so they can see things too.

"Your collective seems to make agreements to incarnate together in difficult periods. The one before Italy was in the era of the Protestant Reformation, and the group again decided that the way to handle the turmoil was to stay very grounded. You all worked the land, did carpentry, and lived in houses. This reading is very different from the others, in that I'm not getting chains of lifetimes about addiction. The main thing that's coming up is this community that you're in. It's like you all have little radio transmitters, even though you're not together, and you tune in to each other."

NORA: "That would explain what happened to me when I was bottoming out. I cried out to God to help me, and these voices came and said, 'We are.' I often feel that I have a lot of help."

ANDREW: "Yes, but I don't think you appreciate the fact that you also GIVE a lot of help. There's this lovingness that's constantly coming out of you in streams, no matter how much pain you're in."

"People in your reincarnational community have used your energy, and you've been drained because you didn't know you had that energy. You reached out to alcohol as a power tool to replenish yourself. But if you recognize and redirect your energy, you can do your own replenishing. You're about to start getting back a great deal of that energy, because the people you've been helping on those other levels are now strong enough to give back. A year from now, life will be entirely different for you, and your pain will be gone."

SUBJECT THREE: BASIL

Basil is a man in his mid-thirties, now sober ten years through AA. He is a chiropractor with an interest in New Age healing methods.

ANDREW channels: "This is not an all-inclusive history of your past lives, only those related to addictions. You are basically a scientist and re-searcher who entered into the pattern of addictions out of curiosity, and then proceeded to explore its many variations and consequences through 2100 years of incarnations. This pattern is one prevalent among people in medicine and other healing fields, and is one reason why there are many addicts in those fields. You are part of a small community of scholars, each conducting research on separate topics. You each work pretty much independently, though you exchange information.

"The decision you made to research the subject of addictions was in 200 BC when you were a scholar, priest, and poet in China. By that time, you'd already had many incarnations and worked out many of the common human problems, with much spiritual development. You were involved with a particular school of poets who made a romance out of drinking and using drugs.You couldn't understand this, as it was alien to your nature, and you felt it was important to understand what it was that appealed to them. On a very, very deep level, you decided to explore it. In that lifetime you simply observed, but this decision extended into many lifetimes, all the way down to today.

"You were next born into a primitive tribe in Indonesia, where the women made a fermented beverage for the men. As one of the women, you chewed up the grains, then spit it into gourds, sealed the gourds over, and then left them to ferment. You were fascinated to learn that there was something in the body that could affect these substances, so that these substances in turn could affect the body in an intoxicating way.

"You had another life as a northern plains Indian in Canada where you were crippled. You were a healer, as you have been many times, but the tribe had a combination of feelings about you, both of awe and of resent-ment at having to take care of you and carry you from place to place. You experimented with mushrooms and other substances to alter conscious-ness, and in those visions, you came through with useful information that was revered long after you were gone. The other experience you needed for your research was that of becoming an addict because someone willed you to be one, a pattern that does happen to many. That was what the tribe did—they willed you into addiction, to cover up for their resentment. They felt if you went deeper and deeper into the substance, you'd produce even more powerful visions, and that they'd be relieved of their resentment. It never evened out and you died early.

"When you get out of these lives, you go back to a place like a study and write down all the information you've compiled. You're trying to find out how human beings can destroy themselves when that is so alien to an animal.

"The next relevant life was as an enormous native woman on a Caribbean island, kind of an old witch working with native plants which you used to have visions. Then the first European traders came through, and you began experimenting with alcohol and blissfully drank yourself to death. You had the ability to be totally detached from your drunkenness, and you did extensive research, many chapters on comparing the effects of these native plants and this chemical substance from over the sea."

BASIL: "Ever the scholar!"

ANDREW: "Yes, indeed. You did discover that the sugar in the alcohol—although you didn't call it that—was far more destructive than anything in the native plants, that anyone who's an alcoholic is also a sugar addict, that it's a dual addiction."

"Following that, you were a ship's doctor on a pirate ship in the 17th century, and you used rum as an anesthetic while you sawed off legs and pulled teeth. Your course of research was to study how the very thing that could relieve pain could also destroy. How was it different when used medicinally than when you drank it to get drunk? You did a lot of research along that line.

"One other factor was that your ship twice went to the same island where you had earlier been the old woman, and while you were there you had incredible visions and knew things you couldn't have known except through past-life memories. It was very confusing because you attributed these visions to the alcohol, and you kept drinking to induce the visions, but they never came except in that one place. In that lifetime, out of loneliness and despair, you did lose sight of the fact that you were doing research. This is a key lifetime to do some work on. You drowned when the ship sank while you were passed out drunk.

"There are other lives in this research project, but one which is interesting isn't exactly a lifetime. You experienced a powerful period of being a fetus during a pregnancy with a black alcoholic prostitute during the later 1800s. You were there very consciously during the whole pregnancy, carefully observing the effects of massive doses of alcohol on the fetus and on the mother's bloodstream. You withdrew abruptly near the end of the pregnancy, because you'd gotten enough information, so the child was stillborn. There was a line of connection—the mother was a descendant of that woman in the Caribbean.

"That brings us to today. You've been doing research in this lifetime too, in the addiction you had to alcohol. But now you've completed the course of research, and it's time for practical application of your knowledge. You will doubtlessly do that in your chiropractic practice, maybe even establishing a clinic for addicted people."

SUBJECT FOUR: DAVID

David is a man in his late thirties who has had a severe weight problem and a life-long addiction to sugar. He is dealing with the sugar addiction and losing weight through Overeaters Anonymous. The reading, which is presented in abridged form, covered many lifetimes of addiction. Only one of his questions is covered here. Both of his parents were alcoholics, and the question was about why David had chosen to be born with this particular father.

ANDREW channels: "There are lines of lifetimes, and you and your father have been together many times. However, this particular pattern seems to have begun when both of you were priests at the end of the Middle Ages in Northern Italy. You were distant cousins and shared a belief in wine as a holy and mystical substance which could be used to induce vision. There were rituals, prayers, and chants priests did while drinking to induce visions. Even today, many priests have a dim memory of this power, and that's one reason why there are so many alcoholic priests.

"You both used wine that way in your meditations, as a positive tool, but it was more positive for you than for him. Often you would have very beautiful visions, and he would have very frightening ones. Yours were about heaven and angels and beautiful music, and his were about the devil. It created jealousy and resentment on both your parts. You felt he was more in touch with the sinner side of himself, that you in your positive visions were not going deep enough, that you were missing out somehow, not really exploring the deeper side of yourself. You considered it a virtue that he could plunge right into his sinful, wicked heart, but of course he didn't consider it positive at all.

"That was an important life for both of you, and the connection between you was very strong. In your current life, you chose to have this alcoholic father to remind yourself of the pattern of addiction you'd gone through in your intervening lives, and in some respects to fulfill the obligation incurred back in that life you shared as priests. You two made a bargain that if you ever figured out the answer to those mystical questions, you'd come back and share them. Before you were born this time, you'd pretty much figured it out, which was the antithesis of that lonely monastery. The answer was that it's not enough to know what God is, you have to teach and help others.

The missing piece was not more knowledge—you both knew enough way back then—the missing piece was using the knowledge. That's what you'll do increasingly in this life—have the knowledge and use it. But in this life you got together with your father out of memory of having made that agreement. There was a magnetic attraction between you and your father, once you were ready to help him. One of the arrangements you made with your father was that you would teach him about balance when he came back, because you went through a different pattern."

DAVID: "Didn't I abdicate that responsibility when I abandoned him in this lifetime, spending years without even talking to him?"

ANDREW: "It takes a moment to teach somebody something. It may take them a thousand years to learn it. You did the teaching, he's still learning, and the teaching hasn't left him. Had you stayed in the relationship, he might never have heard it. You had work to do for yourself, to master your own pattern of addiction. From that experience of your separating from him, there is a very good chance that he heard and that he'll be ready to learn."

"Why your father chose to be an addict in this life is that he was ready to deal with it. He'd had many lifetimes wherein addiction was used to release his violence, and he'd pretty much worked out the violence. He was ready to do the kind of thing you'd already done, which was simply to be a drinker, using it consciously and not to repress things. Often he used it to make himself even more sorrowful, and if he hadn't been a drinker, it might have taken him another lifetime to resolve those issues. Even though it was painful for everyone around him, the drinking helped him get in touch with feelings. Again there was a balance—there was the good side, but there was also damage to him and everyone around him.

"The curious thing about the balancing effect of karma is that you are going to be teaching and helping both addicts and their children, and among the people you help, two of them are going to be the parents of your father when he comes back. You'll be working together to create an atmosphere for him to be born into in which he can completely deal with it, transcend it, and then use the knowledge himself to teach others. It may be many years in the future that this child will be born. You'll probably recognize him, but you don't have to do anything further for him—there's no remaining obligation. He'll work out his patterns through these two people you've helped."

Uncovering Past Life Memories

You may be curious about your own past lives and how they may relate to addiction or to your relationships with addicted people. Some people have spontaneous reincarnational memories, others use the services of psychics, some go through hypnotic regression, but it isn't very difficult for any of us to begin to uncover clues about other lives. In the course of daily living, there are clues like the tips of icebergs pushing through into our conscious awareness. Most of the time we pass right by them, but if we stop and reflect on them, we can begin to uncover those aspects of the psyche which some call past lives.

They may show up as a strong affinity for a particular period of history, or for a culture other than the one into which you were born. For instance, you may have always yearned to go to Ireland, even though you are Jewish and were born in Los Angeles. Or, you may be incapable of passing up Oriental art, even though your family's roots are as slaves on a Georgia plantation. Have you found yourself in a place you've never been before on a trip (or even watching a movie) and had the overwhelming sense that the place is familiar and that you know your way around? Any of these experiences may be a clue to another of your selves. Such powerful attractions and sensations are not idiosyncrasies; they are bonds to these other selves which many call reincarnations.

Often we have dreams in which we see ourselves in other places and other eras. These are probably the most obvious hints of all, but there are also many subtle hints that can lead us to awareness of these other selves. Could you swim from the time you could walk, though no one ever taught you? When you were a child, did you wrap a sheet around yourself and pretend it was a sari? Do you have an instinct for herbal remedies or astrology, although you've never studied them? Do people often jokingly say that you must have been a priestess in another life, or a master chef, or a ballet dancer, or a pickpocket? These are all little hints toward an expanded awareness of self.

If you'd like to stimulate your awareness of these selves, the following process may be useful. Buy a special notebook or a pretty bound book with blank pages. At the top of each page, put down any experiences or memories like the examples given above. The memories will not surface all at once, but the act of buying a notebook with the intention of remembering will help unlock these aspects. Think of the books you read that especially moved you, of dreams that were stirring. Go into childhood in this search, for the child's mind is less bound by the limited horizon we call reality.

For example, you may have written at the top of one page, "I like to buy Japanese vases." Use this as an exploration or meditation. Do you like all such vases or only those from a certain period? Go to the library or a museum and do research. See if you cannot narrow down your sense of what interests you. When you're holding one of your vases, how do you feel? Does it give you a sense of having once made them, or of collecting them, or of selling them? Allow your mind to drift; allow yourself to make up a story. The story may change and keep changing, but trust that your subconscious will ultimately lead you back into a memory. Do you see yourself as having been a Japanese potter in the 16th century? Can you fill your story with relatives, friends, and even enemies?

Or, does your fantasizing take you in a different direction? Perhaps you see yourself as a French countess in the years just before the French Revolution. You were obsessed with things different, new, and foreign, so you had a large collection of Japanese vases. They represented to you everything pure and avant-garde.

An important tool in tracking down past lives can be your dreams. The dream state, like hypnosis, is one in which you can tap into memories and perceptions not readily available to the conscious mind. Dreams are where we return to a fuller consciousness of our spirituality and our visions. Thus, if the waking mind is slow to retrieve reincarnational information, turn your dreams loose on the task.

In order to do this, firmly suggest to yourself each night before going to sleep that you want access to this information. When you wake up, repeat your intention, and then take time to record your dreams. Have the notebook and a pen ready by the bed. If you do this consistently over a period of time, clues or themes will start to accumulate which you can use to augment the notebook work. Eventually, you may find quite direct memories or past life fragments emerging in your dreams and meditations. In the bibliography you will find several books on dreams listed that can help you deepen into this process.

Some people can tap into past life selves by gazing into a mirror in a darkened room with only a tiny light or candle behind you. As you stare into the mirror, without blinking if you can, you may find your face shifting into other faces of both sexes, portraying people that you have been.

There are also stones and essences which can help you in this quest THYME, which has to do with experiencing time differently, is useful. The combination of STAR TULIP, CALIFORNIA POPPY and YARROW is a good one, in that STAR TULIP helps you open up psychically and CALIFORNIA POPPY brings out past life abilities, while YARROW keeps you balanced in the process and provides psychic shielding. Other remedies specifically said to work on past life information are FOUR LEAF CLOVER, HENNA, and GREEN ROSE. As for stones, the best would be a clear quartz crystal ball or egg, into which you would gaze by candlelight. Lapis is legendary as a help in psychic work, but Katrina Raphaell says it also helps to cleanse old memory patterns with emotional charges on them.

EXERCISE: A Technique for Past Life Recall

If you're not getting anywhere with these general tips, the following is an exercise which, when practiced regularly, should get results for you.

Sit in your bubble with your eyes closed. Become aware of your breathing.

Feel that there is a large 3-D movie screen on the outside of your bubble. Create it, in detail, in your imagination.

Feel that you can program your third eye, your brow chakra, to beam out onto that screen scenes from other lives. You might program it by saying, "Core Self, I want to see scenes from my past lives. I want to see scenes that will help me understand my addiction and heal it."

When images come to the surface, do not become attached to them. If you have any emotional responses to them, use the exercises in Chapter Six to work through them.

Getting Perspective on Past Life Memories

If you've succeeded in seeing some of your past lives but you don't like what you saw, do not take them too seriously. For instance, we all die in each of our lives, and we've all had accidents or illnesses which brought about those deaths. Focusing on the manner of death, then, is giving it too much importance. After all, you're alive now, aren't you? Use the memories as a way of learning a lesson to help you be a better person in this life, rather than being too concerned or guilty about what you did or didn't do in some other life. It's never too late to correct our faults and flaws. We're given these memories to teach us, not to chastise us. If the purpose of reincarnation is to give each individual soul every kind of experience, then we've all been soldiers, priests, artisans, healers, and prostitutes. We've all misused power, all killed and been killed. The point of having all these experiences—and the point of remembering them—is to grow from them and become greater. That way we don't have to repeat the mistakes of our past lives.

CHAPTER THREE

COFFEE, CAFFEINE ADDICTION
AND THE WORLD OF WORK

We all have addictions, some of which are viewed as major while others are laughed off as minor. A case in point is the caffeine addiction that is practically universal. Even children who are "too young" to drink coffee drink caffeinated sodas. Would-be sophisticates make a fetish of getting the finest beans and brewing them the precise way, just as others make a fetish of getting the correct vintage wine to go with their chosen entre.

Coffee is made from the roasted, brewed seeds of the evergreen coffee plant. The plant requires a moist, hot climate and rich soil. It was known to be used before 1000 AD in Ethiopia, by the Fifteenth Century in Arabia, and by the middle of the Seventeenth Century, it had reached most of Europe and had been introduced into the Americas. The caffeine found in coffee is a stimulant when used in moderation. It can cause irritability, depression, insomnia, indigestion, and if used in excess can eventually lead to heart irregularities and delirium.

Caffeine and the World of Work

Caffeine addiction is a subset of workaholism. Almost all coffee-holics are workaholics, for there is no other reason to be wired up that way. We use caffeine as a power tool to alter the body's natural rhythms in order to overproduce. Even children are under enormous pressure today to produce and compete, so they drink cola until they are "old enough" for coffee. Traditional coffee break times are geared toward valleys in the normal daily biorhythm. We no longer respect these rhythms or our bodies' limits. We live in artificially heated and lighted environments where we are losing touch with Moon/Sun cycles and seasonal rhythms. It used to be that the earth and all the life forms on it rested in winter. In common with all life forms on earth, we are cells in the body of the planet, so we go through a natural slowdown at night and in the winter. With the other stimulants, we bypass the slower parts of our rhythms to keep on producing all day and all year around.

Coffee is the vision-in-work tool, which is how coffee breaks got institutionalized. Coffee addicts are looking for a vision or purpose in their work—the job, schoolwork, housework, or even work on the self. Most work is so devoid of vision as to be unrewarding. At some point, people give up expecting to find vision in their work. "If I cannot find it," the coffee addict says, "at least let me find the energy to do what I have to do." Energy is no substitute for vision, and coffee is no substitute for satisfaction in work, no matter how perfectly it's brewed.

Humanity Gears up for Off-World Living

Humans, at least those who are residents of earth, are at a peculiar place in their development, and this explains why work is no longer a source of satisfaction. Just as the womb no longer holds and nourishes the fetus after it reaches a particular stage of development, Terra no longer holds us. We've passed the stage where being earthbound is satisfying; we yearn, however unconsciously, for the stars. The kinds of work which sustained us on earth are no longer enough. Coffee consoles us, helps us continue in the despised work still required to sustain life here on earth in the interim.

On a broader level, outside waking consciousness, we're using coffee to free ourselves from the earth and the current human form, to be able to adapt to off-world living. Coffee is the milk which will wean us from Mother Earth. We're preparing to live on planets where the diurnal cycle is different than 24 hours. Coffee is used, though not consciously, to simulate the different biorhythms of such planets. Here there aren't enough hours in the day and enough daylight hours in the year to realize our visions.

We're a generation of those with new visions, and we use coffee to boost us along, to sustain us in pushing for the desired result. Those who become addicted and sensitized to coffee are those who have already made the mental body change but don't have the physical capacity. Coffee addicts are those who see how life will be in the age to come and who are determined to function that way now, without the proper vehicle. Caffeine abuse is the consequence of living in an era when the mind and spirit are reaching forward into a new era, while the vehicle is still rooted in the old one.

The proper vehicle for carrying out such visions will be developed as human form continues to evolve. We're subjected to many kinds of energy bombardment on earth today. All are designed to contribute to that development, which will at first be called mutation. The current Terran form is the immature larva, a stage in the development of the full human form. Terran form is fully life-sustaining, yet as incomplete as the caterpillar is to the butterfly. Understand that all life forms are intelligent and are part of the ever-evolving plan of the Universe. No life-form/indwellingness is wasted; all living is learning, so DNA is learning and developing even as we are. Even cancer cells are part of that development. We'll find the cure for cancer when this phase of growth and experimenting is over.

The fetus of a pregnant coffee abuser—even and especially those who miscarry—is also part of the experimentation. In years to come, we'll become as concerned about the fetal caffeine syndrome as we now are about the fetal alcohol syndrome. For instance, some hyperactive children are actually the products of this syndrome. The fetus of even a moderate coffee drinker is partaking in this evolution, the DNA changing to accept the altered biorhythm of the mother/host. The fretful, overactive infant arising from such a pregnancy simply suffers from an immature vehicle not yet coordinated; as an adult, the same hyperactivity can be productively channeled. From the longer viewpoint, it's all part of the evolution toward off-world living, toward universal belongingness.

If this set of ideas seems far-fetched and millennia from realization, it is because earthlings have yet to even master the one-world stage, still being entrenched in the babyhood that nationalism represents. A life form which is still mired in racial hatred is too primitive to live in comfort with life forms whose differences don't stop with color or language. Universal communication through the media is the most powerful tool of the vision of the oneness of humankind. Some of the visions caffeine abusers are currently bringing into being will propel us into uniworldability and almost simultaneously into the mutliworldedness of which we're speaking. The one-hundredth monkey will be a space voyager.

Women, Their Cycles, Men, and Caffeine

As Donna has explored in her book, *Being A Lunar Type In A Solar World*, today's career woman is pressured to function like a man, productive and rational in all phases of her monthly biorhythm. For both men and women, coffee addiction is a tool to suppress feminine traits and create an individual who functions as a hyper-masculine, aggressive work machine—the kind that operates at high speed until it is rendered obsolete by a newer class of human, at which point it drops dead of heart failure.

The period of introversion, rest, and reflection that older cultures provided for the menstruating woman is now seen as archaic and sexist, even though it was designed with considerable wisdom for the feminine vehicle. Women use coffee to override the menstrual cycle, to continue to be productive and clear-headed all month long. Yet due to the difference in hormone levels premenstrually, women are hypersensitive to coffee at that point, especially in the lethal sugared black coffee form. Observe yourself and notice how that cup of coffee after dinner is fine at some times of the month and at others keeps you up half the night. Caffeine interacts strongly with estrogen and other hormones, and thus affects you differently at different points of the hormonal cycle.

On a less aware level, women have also used caffeine and other stimulants like nicotine to lengthen their reproductive life and delay menopause. This development of the past few decades is a stage in the evolution of the superhuman. The ultimate vehicle will have less differentiation between the sexes, as such psychophysical differences no longer serve us and in fact impede our progress. Women who train athletically or diet until they lose their cycles are also unconsciously working on this change in vehicle. The current fitness/thinness com-pulsion, despite its tendency toward distortion, is also part of it. Gay people who are androgynous are also part of the evolution.

Similarly, the male body is being subtly femininized by the long-term effect of introducing massive amounts of estrogen into eggs, chicken, and other meats and by the proliferation of sugar in our diet. None of this change is due to conscious spiritual awareness on the part of the industrial/financial elite—all they know is that they sell more products that way—but the end result is cooperation in the evolutionary plan. How confusing and paradoxical it is that the most crass of conscious motives sometimes makes a more tangible contribution toward the overall evolution than does the highest, most noble of motives.

The Physical and Emotional Effects of Caffeine Addiction

All of the above ideas aren't meant to glorify coffee or caffeine any more than we glorify any other kind of drug. Addiction of any form brings suffering. We all know what it is to be a bit wired from too much coffee, but the true addict is so continually wired up as to never know a moment of peace. The emotional consequences of the addiction are anxiety, eventually to the extreme of panic attacks. Many caffeine-addicted people are paying a great deal of money for psychotherapy—and may even be taking tranquilizers for their unease, anxiety, irritability, and depression without realizing their unhappiness is the result of far too much caffeine. Many also wind up with a secondary habit of taking sleeping pills, smoking a joint or two, or having a few drinks at night to shut down the day's overstimulation by caffeine. Like all addictions, this one is subject to denial, so the abuser who needs sleeping pills to shut down at night blames it on the stress of the job.

What happens physically is that every organ and every system in the body is stimulated to overproduce. In particular, the heart and the adrenal glands gear up in response to stress, in the well-known fight-or-flight response, and caffeine affects the adrenals profoundly, and the pancreas as well. We live in a stressful world for which no maps, no guidelines, and no certainties exist. Part of the stress is that our physical vehicle was designed for a more earth-bound, pastoral life style. Our hyper-adrenalized life styles are an addiction all their own--an addiction to excitement, a world full of stimulation junkies. We use caffeine to gear up to live in the stress. Yet caffeine increases the adrenal response and thus ultimately stresses the adrenals themselves, causing us to live in a perpetual state of readiness for fight or flight, thus the anxiety and irritability.

What is addiction varies from individual to individual, but anything over three cups of coffee a day will doubtlessly affect your peace of mind. The body's capacity to tolerate caffeine also breaks down over time, and you become sensitized to it, so there comes a point at which three cups of coffee a day triggers the same kind of overstimulation that ten cups once did. Physical withdrawal from caffeine can be surprisingly hard, varying from extreme lethargy, irritability, and depression for the heavy abuser to such puzzling effects as constipation and menstrual cycle disruption for the lighter user. Like any stimulant, the rebound effect on withdrawal is a period of depressed functioning of every part of the system.

Coffee and the Chakras

The chakra most strongly affected by caffeine is the solar plexus, the seat of the ego or sense of self. Many of the kinds of work people do today are far more demanding and challenging than work was in the past, and thus far more given to self-doubt. Corporate employment is also much more involved with management and relating to different levels of authority than physical labor was. Coffee breaks are about expanding your power. In order to let go of coffee, you'd need to cleanse and strengthen your solar plexus chakra regularly. It would also be wise to shield your solar plexus at work, perhaps by imaging a wide golden cummerbund around the solar plexus while you are there. In particularly challenging situations, such as an evaluation or a presentation, you might tape a small crystal on that area.

It's no accident that coffee became popular on a global level at the same time that imperialism spread through the world. On one hand, the conquerors brought coffee with them wherever they went. On the other hand, they also took solar plexus wounding in their treatment of those they conquered—and their own self-doubt about their mastery. You think it's easy being a Mem Sahib? We'll see again and again, as we consider the various substances, that addiction and enslavement are a pair of phenomena, partners in crime so to speak. Although overt enslavement is no longer so manifest in the world, its heritage of addiction goes on for generations, transmitted both by learned behavior patterns and by the subtle alterations in gene structure that habitual chemical abuse creates.

Coffee also affects the third eye and root chakras. At its best, coffee is a tool for generating grounded yet visionary work by linking root and third eye energies to the solar plexus. When our ancestors were nomadic or when work was all done at home, in the form of farming and handicrafts, it was easier to make that connection. As the age of exploration and then industrialization separated the work place from the home, this tool became more and more popular. While it initially stimulates these three chakras positively, it eventually overstimulates them and causes them to shut down. One drinks more, in the hope of reawakening those energies.

Rather than coffee, you might try this exercise to activate the connections. You can do it at your desk at work. Sit quietly. Place your right palm over your root chakra and your left on your forehead. Feel the energy circulating between those two points in your body. When the energy is moving easily, bring both palms over your solar plexus. Inhale and exhale deeply three times, and then go back to work.

Other Caffeinated Drinks

Most of this chapter is about coffee, but several other substances, all with less frequent addictive patterns, also contain caffeine. Teas from the tea plant—an evergreen native of India and perhaps China and Japan, a relative of the camillia—has been used for thousands of years, and is another of these products. Tea was being produced on a commercial scale in China by the 8th century, and was introduced into Europe and then in the Americas in the 17th century by Dutch merchants. The caffeine content of tea is less than that of coffee. Black teas, pekoes, are fermented before being marketed, oolongs are partially fermented, while green teas are not. Each of these processes slightly effects the power properties of the beverage brewed from the dried leaves.

Tea is milder than coffee, but its effects on the body if consumed in large amounts are similar. On an energy level tea affects the conscious mind in a slightly different way. Whereas coffee supports the world of work and energizes one to integrate vision into the work place, tea has the opposite effect. It tends to draw a veil between vision and work, encourages contemplation separate from action, affecting the same chakras but in different ways. All we have to do to understand this is to think of the difference between a coffee break and a tea ceremony, a ritual whose effect is not one cultivated by our society. Many of us drink tea, but we aren't encouraged to use it as a power tool, only as a stimulant.

Cola, a tropical tree native to Africa, produces pods that also contain caffeine. Cola nuts are chewed for its effect, and are also exported for use in soft drinks and medicines. We consume vast amounts of cola-containing products in this country, but it's hard to tell how much of that is caffeine addiction and how much is sugar addiction. So if you find yourself a cola addict, you might also want to read through the information on sugar. Hard drinks like coffee and soft drinks like sodas are similar in their effects, with cola products creating a softer work impulse that makes them popular with students and younger individuals.

The cacao tree, a native of South America, produces pods that are fermented, and whose extracted seeds, called coca beans, are used to make the cocoa from which chocolate is derived. All cacao products contain caffeine. Chocolate is produced by blending roasted cocoa beans with sugar, cocoa butter, and milk solids, so as with cola addiction, chocolate addication is also related to sugar abuse. A chocolate drink prepared by the Aztecs was introduced to Europe by the Spanish invaders in the 16th century. Today it is used all over the planet. If colas and coffee encouraged work, and tea helps to disconnect one from it, chocolate is used as a reward for work, and as a substitute for the major work-alternative that our culture allows us—love. A chemical found in chocolate is said to also be produced by our brains when we are in love.

Mate, yerba mate, or Paraguay tea, is brewed from the leaves and shoots of an evergreen tree in the holly family that grows in South America. Although little used in the U.S. or Europe, it is the most popular beverage in much of South America, and contains more caffeine than tea from the tea plant does. Its effect on the body is similar to that of coffee. Its effect on our state of consciousness is somewhere between that of coffee and tea, in that it separates one from the work drive, but not so widely as tea does.

The Recovering Addict and Caffeine

At meetings of A.A. and other Anonymous programs, they usually serve plenty of strong coffee, often with sugar and cookies. The drinking of large amounts of coffee is often misguidedly encouraged by other members as a harmless substitute for what they've given up. Recovering alcoholics and other addicts often turn to caffeine to sustain the high they're missing. It's an understandable yet destructive attempt to self-medicate out of the depression that is a natural, healing process in recovery. Once substance abuse stops, the body slows down in order to mend itself. Rest is a better healer, yet it's hard to work, make ninety meetings in ninety days, spend time with your loved ones, and still get plenty of rest. The abuser believes coffee makes that juggling act possible. Yet this practice so easily leads to caffeine abuse and addiction, with the kind of suffering described above.

There's a puzzling phenomenon in the Twelve-Step groups of members who work their programs hard and are doing their all to recover, yet who seem to be wretchedly miserable all the time. This may go on for long periods, despite the help of therapy and formal addiction treatment programs. Other members weary of hand-holding through the agony these people suffer and wind up shaking their heads. These unfortunate sufferers get labelled as mentally disturbed. No one inquires how much caffeine or tobacco they're using, for we're all in denial about their power. As a rule of thumb, a recovering addict who is often miserable after the first year or so is generally someone who has taken on another addiction, whether it's compulsive debt, sex, sugar abuse or caffeine. Never underestimate the power of even your smallest addiction to rob you of peace of mind.

The Habit-Transforming Diagram for Coffee

In our earlier book, we introduced the idea of the habit-transforming diagram as one tool for giving up your addiction. Habits such as addictions are imprinted on our brain circuits in the same way as computer circuits get wired. To stop a habit, you need to erase and rewire the circuit, and that's what these diagrams are for.

The diagram for coffee is printed on the following page. In order to use it, look up and down between the vertical parallel lines at the center of the diagram about 25 times. You could xerox a copy to take to work with you and use it each time you felt the need for a cup of coffee. Use it at least three to five times a day.

The Right Use of Coffee

While coffee is a tool for releasing work energy, it is often abused. It's not a food, and its repeated introduction into the digestive tract is a violation of the territorial integrity of our inner organs. However, infrequent use can be an aid to stimulating the body to work efficiently. The following is a nondamaging way of using coffee if you feel you cannot give it up.

EXERCISE: Follow these steps:

Brew a small amount of coffee, grinding it by hand if possible. Instant coffee will not do. Brew a quarter of a cup to half a cup maximum.

Sit in a quiet place, in your bubble of white light. Sit looking out a window if possible, not looking at anything in particular so much as staring out into space, and very slowly sip the coffee.

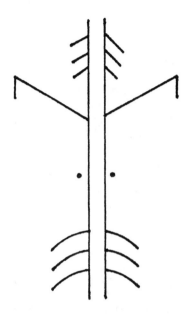

HABIT TRANSFORMING DIAGRAM

FOR COFFEE

As the coffee enters your body, feel it drop down into your energy channel until it reaches the root chakra. When it gets there, it will release a tremendously beautiful orange light. This orange light will provide you with all the energy you need.

Feel this energy spread out through your entire body, and feel that you can store some in your solar plexus.

When you feel energized, dissolve the bubble and return to work. Whenever you need a pick-me-up, don't return to the coffee machine, return to the orange light that was released by the coffee in this exercise. Don't do this more than once a day.

The light substitute and the essences and stones given below would serve you still better than even this limited use of coffee. An intermediate step would be to roll brewed coffee on your palms and absorb it through your hands. The vibration goes right to where you need it.

EXERCISE: A Coffee Substitute, A Work Tool

This meditation is helpful for anyone who feels the need for more energy for working in the world, at the job or in creative work. It will serve as a light alternative to a cup of coffee, except that there's no actual coffee involved, it's quite similar to the one just learned, which might serve as a stage in the process of giving up coffee.

Follow these steps:

Sit in your bubble of white light. Relax all your muscles, in your face and from the neck on down.

Each time you inhale, see a thin but bright column of glowing orange light enter through the top of your head. With each breath you inhale, draw it further and further down your spinal column.

When the orange light reaches the tip of your spine, the coccyx, it will release energy, which will flow out from it in waves of orange light.

Each time you inhale, the orange light from the coccyx will travel out into your body until it has filled every part of it.

When your body is filled with orange light, glowing, and feeling vital, affirm that you've indeed opened to the place within you to hold the energy needed to carry on with your work, your solar plexus chakra.

Dissolve the bubble and go back to what you were doing. See if you indeed have more energy to work with. Repeat whenever needed, with once an hour being the maximum dosage.

If you're tired and feeling draggy, physical exercise is also helpful in re-energizing. A half hour of aerobic exercise would work wonders. One of those small round trampolines would do the trick nicely.

Essences and Stones to Help Replace Coffee

The flower remedies can be very useful in cutting back on coffee. The COFFEE flower essence eases caffeine addiction and works strongly on the mental body for decision making. If you took a drop of the diluted essence each time you wanted a cup of coffee, your need for caffeine would change. The TEA plant is also available as an essence and might help tea drinkers, but we've no knowledge of its functioning. LEMON is useful for the mental body and is a specific against caffeine addiction. If the need for caffeine is arising out of a solar plexus problem, SUN-FLOWER helps balance the ego, while various essences such as SELF-HEAL, GENTIAN, and LARCH help with self-doubt.

There are a number of essences related to energy and to fatigue. The most crucial are HORNBEAM, OLIVE, and OAK, each dealing with a type of exhaustion, in order from the least to the most. What Donna has noticed, in periods of having to use them over the years due to exhaustion, is that after a while you get smarter and cut back on the coffee without really thinking about it. You learn something about conserving your energy and resting so that you don't work yourself to the verge of collapse.

A number of the essences discussed in our earlier book in reference to realizing your visions would also help the caffeine addict: ELM if you are overwhelmed by the challenges and tend to give up easily. The BLACK-BERRY, MADIA, and IRIS combination is, once more, excellent for manifesting your vision, with MADIA being the ingredient that helps you to focus and concentrate. SHOOTING STAR might help the would-be space traveller deal with the alienation, however unconscious, of being physically stuck on earth while the heart yearns for the stars.

There's also a crystal substitute for coffee and other caffeinated products. You'll need a chunk of amethyst about the size of a grape and a piece of dark green tourmaline about the same size or a little smaller. Hold the amethyst in your left hand and the tourmaline in your right. Feel the pulsations of energy emanating from the two stones and let it spread throughout your body, merging and filling it with power. Feel that you can hold this energy in your chest and move out from it. You can also carry these stones with you—best if you have two pockets and put the stones on their proper side.

Stones for the solar plexus would help replace caffeine. Try taping malachite, peridot, green tourmaline, or a clear quartz crystal on the solar plexus when you sleep—or when you're in a situation which threatens to wound your self-esteem. Be sure to cleanse the stone thoroughly afterwards.

CHAPTER FOUR

TOBACCO:
THE BRIDGE BETWEEN CHAKRAS

What Tobacco Is

Tobacco is a plant in the nightshade family, which includes white potatoes, red peppers, eggplant, tomatoes, petunias, mandrake, and belladonna or deadly nightshade. Native to tropical America, tobacco is a large-leafed perennial which is usually cultivated as an annual. It requires a warm climate and rich, well-drained soil. After being picked, the leaves are cured, fermented, and aged for use in cigarettes, cigars, snuff, pipes, and chewing tobacco.

The use of tobacco originated with natives of the Americas before Columbus. It was introduced into Spain and Portugal in the mid-Sixteenth Century, and its growth spread from there to the Middle East and Far East. The nicotine in tobacco is responsible for its effects, and has, along with the tars and carbon monoxide in tobacco smoke, been found to be cancer-forming. Nicotine is a stimulant to all body systems. When the cigarette smoker withdraws from nicotine, there is a period of many months when the system is slowed down in order to repair itself. The heart and lungs are very damaged by a long, heavy cigarette habit. Since sugar is added to manufactured cigarettes, a cigarette smoker may also have a sugar habit. Manufactured cigarettes also contain various chemicals which affect the physical and energy body in unknown ways and which need to be removed from the system.

Smoking and Dreaming

Cigarette addicts don't know how to dream, by which we mean the faculty for their dreams to work for them has been lost, forgotten, or damaged. Lighting the fire, the spiraling smoke, are metaphors for the process of dreaming, whereby imagination sparks one's life experiences. These experiences, though contained, are transformed into the free-flowing billows of pure dreaming. We deal with our day to day problems through dream work. Anyone who smokes is having trouble in the dream world.

Initially, smoking heightens daytime perceptions which should stimulate the catalogue of images used in dreamwork. Ultimately, just as smoking deadens the taste buds, it also deadens the senses. One smokes more and more in hopes of getting back that initial burst of heightened perceptions. The real burst is to be found in dream work. Later, we'll give suggestions for strengthening your relationship to dreams, so you can use them more consciously. Marijuana is also related to dreaming, but, because it's a stronger drug, is dealt with separately in the next chapter.

The Holy Functions and Ancient Rites of Smoking

Fire was recognized by the ancients as a changer and releaser of the power of certain substances. It makes things more yang, therefore active rather than passive, and it releases the essence of the substance. Thus the ancients burned or smoked a variety of things. Tobacco was only one, a stimulant, but there were also depressants. There were plants smoked for different parts of the body, healing and balancing them. There were different smokes for different folks and for different times of the year, depending on what was needed for that season. Incenses, too, served a similar function, releasing things within us by their aromas. For those who wish to stop smoking, it would help to indulge in the wonderful diversity of incense available today and to experiment to see which ones are most calming to you.

Today we forget to smoke a variety of things, and many of these plants are extinct or their properties forgotten. We are hung up on the stimulant properties of nicotine. It promises to cut through the overwhelming number of vibrations we must deal with today, like an eraser that cleans the slate. It puts us in a different mind state, wiping out thought. This is a legitimate need, but, by wiping the slate, tobacco only serves to prepare you for talking with spirit guides, nature spirits, and beings on other levels of consciousness. It prepares you, but it does not open you to hearing that guidance. Today, however, there is little support and less preparation for such guidance; most of us, in fact, run from it.

For that kind of guidance, other ingredients were added. Tobacco was generally only 5-10% of the smoking mixture. Plants native to different parts of the world were designed by nature spirits to meet the special needs of the people and animals native to the area. Different tribes made use of different plants, depending on what grew locally and why the ceremony was being done. For rituals of various seasons and kinds, the shamans knew which plants to use. Sage, of which there are thirty distinctly different kinds, was considered especially useful in women's rituals. Among the other common ingredients were lavender, sassafras, juniper, elderberry bark, sun grass, sweet grass, dried willow bark, and other plants with mind-altering properties.

Smokers don't know that those other ingredients are needed, but use tobacco by itself to wipe out the overstimulation in our environment. They use it to try to focus and center themselves, as a tool against the fragmentation that exists in our lives today. Then they get frustrated that it doesn't work and smoke more and more to get the desired effect, all futilely. Sage and tobacco are a far more effective combination than tobacco alone, since sage is what moves you to that other level of consciousness. Even today, a wise person is called a sage, in a trace memory of this plant's effect. Simply burning sage in your room, as the Native Americans still do, helps greatly. It purifies the environment, also, of negative energy soaked up in the course of living.

In the rituals of preparation, tobacco and other substances the ancients used for consciousness altering were changed, purified, and heightened. They were gathered with reverence by shamans and herbalists who knew their power and who knew when they were ripe. This reverent touching brought out something that today's mechanical gathering by disgruntled field workers is lacking. These substances used to be dried in the sun, which is, after all, a highly potent form of light, whereas tobacco is now dried in barns. Prayer and invocation of spirits used to begin the smoking ceremonies. Today we invoke nothing, except perhaps, "Oh, God, how can I get through this?" None of these human ingredients are present in today's cigarettes, only chemically processed tobacco and sugar. So we smoke more and more and get less and less of what we are looking for.

The stones from which pipes were traditionally made were themselves transmuters of the the energy of tobacco and other smoked substances, part of the ritual and part of what made them effective. They acted as crucibles for releasing the essence of the plant. Pipesmokers who make a fetish of collecting pipes dimly remember this. In different parts of the world, different plants were burned, and different stones were used for the pipes. Meerschaum might have been used in one area, flint in another, and ivory elsewhere. In Black Elk's book, *The Sacred Pipe*, the smoking rites of one group, the Souix, are discussed. (Penguin Metaphysical Library, 1971, NY.)

The stones naturally occurring in an area acted on the native plants to meet the needs of the native dwellers. Orientals used jade and alabaster as containers for their incense, not just because such containers were lovely to behold, but also because they worked with the substances they burned. Native Americans traditionally use abalone shells to burn sage. If you burn sage, other incense, or tobacco, you might do well to imitate our spiritual elders and burn them in stone holders.

Another lost part of the holiness of smoking is that it was mostly done in a group, in ceremony, as a way of bonding with one another. Native Americans, tobacco users, did this until their culture was so fragmented by our own that it got lost, except for a few who preserve the wisdom. Smoking in a group, in ceremony, was a way of mixing and joining energies with one another, all inhaling the same smoke. At the end of a tribal war, the passing of a peace pipe was a way of cementing a bond, of letting go of differences. The fundamental unity of the Red race was underlined by the fact that all tribes, friend or foe, smoked ritual pipes made from the same red stone found only in one place in Minnesota.

Today we try to get the same effect of group bonding in solitary puffing. We are confused that the easing of isolation and alienation does not happen. Politicians in smoke filled rooms still have their own rituals. They still smoke together, passing around cigars as a way of trying to make peace among warring factions and conflicting interests.

The Making of the Marlboro Man

You may have noticed that, with one notable exception, many of the cigarette commercials seem to focus on a macho, even wild west image of smoking as a he-man pursuit. Even Virginia Slims, the cigarette that boasts to women about how far they've come, details the way women who smoked in the past were considered unfeminine and ostracized. How did this Western civilization equation of smoking with masculinity come about? We learned to smoke tobacco from the Native Americans of this continent with, as we will see, a variety of consequences.

What the Paleface male saw, in what may only loosely be called diplomatic dealings with Native Americans was the male ritual of smoking. The European alien was not party to such personal and private questions as whether women smoked, what they smoked, and when they smoked. Women had their own group rituals, their own consciousness-altering devices, and their own special times of pursuing them, but the European did not see them. Thus, this mysterious drug, tobacco, was seen as a male prerogative and doubtlessly part of what made the Native American so fierce. The passing out of cigars by the new father is a hold-over of such rituals, a group partaking of his masculinity in poorly-disguised phallic symbolism.

Wet Dreams and Waking Visions

Young people seem to equate smoking with being grown up. There is tremendous social pressure to smoke as a way of seeming cool and "with it." This is because young people share a race memory that long ago the first joining with the tribe to smoke ritually was one of the rites of passage. Teens have always wanted to belong, and today's teen dimly remembers that smoking was somehow part of belonging, but confuses the symbolic act of smoking with actually taking one's place in the tribe. Adolescence was not so prolonged in a less complicated time when 15 and 16 year olds were full adult members of society and were equipped to take on adult tasks. The smoker WAS a grown up and ready to become a part of the group.

In that earlier era, sexual initiation and spiritual initiation proceeded hand in hand. The physiological and hormonal changes of puberty happened along with the opening into other levels of consciousness. Wet dreams and waking visions developed at about the same time. As young people began to have some awareness of the other dimensions, they would be initiated into the rituals of smoking which opened the consciousness even further. Today's young people somehow dimly remember that smoking was somehow a rite of passage into adulthood. Yet, if you start smoking and still don't feel grownup and don't assume adult re-sponsibilities, smoking is empty of meaning. You may smoke more and more as the addiction progresses, yet still feel empty and purposeless.

How the Red Race Gave Tobacco to the European

When Native Americans introduced tobacco to the European immigrants, they deliberately left out sage and some of the other crucial consciousness-altering ingredients. On one hand, it was because of a spiritual principle of not introducing consciousness-altering substances to the spiritually unawakened. Native Americans quickly saw that, although the Europeans had been through puberty and were technically adults, they suffered from a curious and rather tragic spiritual retardation. Europeans did not see visions, could not communicate with their ancestors in spirit, and did not sense the divinity in the earth and her four elements. Not only did they have these perceptual disabilities, from which the occasional Native American also suffered, but they also arrogantly ridiculed those who could perceive such things. Clearly Europeans were not ready for smoking rituals, except perhaps on a melodrama level, much as the European's own church rituals had deteriorated into empty ceremonies.

An additional reason why the Native American gave the European tobacco without sage was as a kind of biochemical warfare, hoping to weaken this powerful enemy by erasing parts of consciousness. Tobacco without sage blurs part of consciousness, yet does not open the door to other dimensions for insight into solving problems. Many have observed how the Europeans subdued Native Americans by addicting them to alcohol, but few have remarked on the more subtle and yet powerfully insidious addiction to tobacco Native Americans visited on their captors. Addiction and enslavement are twin strains of history, and you hardly find one without the other. The exchange of vices between oppressor and oppressed goes on and on.

Part of Native American history is that of savage wars between tribes. Many of the Europeans who came to America and perpetrated their brutality on Native Americans were actually reincarnations of vanquished tribal enemies. Vindictive even beyond death, they came back as a still more powerful aggressor, equipped with gunpowder, to repay the destruction of their own tribes by others in the wars between tribes. Karma balances out in the end. Those who ravaged the Red race will also pay.

Part of the generation gap between parent and young person in the Sixties came about because many of the young people coming of age in that era, especially those drawn to consciousness-altering substances, were Native Americans in their most recent incarnations. They remembered the exploitation by which white America came into being and deeply desired to change our consciousness. Having been so deeply affected by violence, and having learned the lesson that there will always be somebody with bigger and better weapons, they wished to change our consciousness nonviolently. There were few Native American bodies to incarnate into, due to the genocide of that race, so people with this incarnational history were drawn into the bodies of descendants of those early settlers.

Those who are drawn to study the wisdom and healing arising from Native American teachings are also likely to have had Native American lives and to have as one of their life tasks the preservation of this wisdom. Many heavy tobacco smokers, as well as marijuana users, are also puzzled former Native Americans, seeking to draw upon the lost wisdom, and one of the ways of getting out of smoking may be to study those teachings.

Tobacco's Effects on the Chakras

The nature of smoke is to move freely, building bridges between different points in the reality structure. In the body, tobacco creates bridges between different chakras, bridges that shift and bend at different times. The root chakra is involved. Notice how you can light up a cigarette anytime, anyplace, and feel at home with yourself for a moment.

The solar plexus can become involved. Think of all those smoke-filled conference rooms, with people using their solar plexus energy for the work process. Obviously the throat chakra is involved, as the throat is the entryway into the body of this substance, so there's an attempt to open up communication—to have a pow-wow. The third eye is part of this bridging, intuitive flashes emerging from this smoky cloud of the unconscious. Those who inhale smoke second-hand, such as the children of heavy smokers, also experience these shifts in consciousness routinely, growing up without clear awareness that this shifting is not the usual way of functioning.

Tobacco allows the energies of all the chakras to be interwoven. Root to brow, throat to root, solar plexus to root, constantly shifting and changing. People who use it to stimulate only one chakra will find themselves disappointed, yet sensing that this chakra IS affected, they wind up smoking more, only to get further lost on this ever-shifting bridge. When you feel alienated at work, a cigarette will deepen your root chakra connection, but at any moment it may carry you off to third eye awareness. When you need to communicate better, you light up, but find yourself instead in a solar plexus mode of expression, acting egotistical and pushy with the boss you really only wanted to communicate with. Far better for chakra dancing is the exercise in Chapter Seven on building links between chakras. If you're still smoking, especially, use that exercise until you can build the chain in an instant, and do it when ever you feel tempted to smoke.

Tobacco's Shifts in Popularity

We have immersed ourselves in a cloud of smoke, have puffed ourselves silly over the past seventy or eighty years. Now there is a vast movement afoot to ban smoking from public places, and there's nearly as much social pressure on people to stop smoking as there was once on people to start. There is even the rise of a certain kind of judgement about people who smoke. The Center for Disease Control reports a five percent drop in the number of smokers in just one year, between 1986 and 1987. It's no accident that the surgeon general has mandated printed warnings about the physical damage done by cigarettes. We are headed toward an anti-smoking era nearly as pronounced as the Prohibition era's anti-alcohol stance.

The change is coming about because mass smoking has already made the changes for which we needed tobacco—whether to the smoker or to those who "only" inhaled it second-hand from the polluted air. Now we need a balance, and the fad for smoking is ready to recede. The fad was actually the collective unconscious pull toward tobacco's effects on the energy body, weaving bridges between the chakras. Such rising and falling in popularity of various addictions signal a culture's collective decision to use/abuse/forsake that particular drug's effect on the various bodies and on the culture as a whole. Thus, addictions come and go. Tobacco has had its day, and it is now nearly obsolete. Perhaps in time it will recede to its original ritual use, or perhaps it will become one of those extinct or forgotten plants.

Why Does Cigarette Smoking Cause Cancer?

Not everyone who smokes gets cancer, but most everyone who smokes these days is either worried about cancer or busy denying that they worry about it. Yes, it is true that the chemicals in today's tobacco create an irritation of body systems and that the smoke irritates the lungs, contributing to cancer on the physical level. Yet the metaphysical level is the real genesis of any disease, the disturbance happening there long before changes occur on the physical level. The lack of reverence in its use and the loss of the protection afforded by the group ritual is one of the contributing factors. More important, however, is the anger that tobacco doesn't do any longer what it promises. We all have a race memory of what smoking was for, and no matter how much the smoker smokes, the end result is missing. The frustration over not getting to that place in consciousness, not getting what is needed, is poisonous to the system.

Healing the Effects of Smoke or Industrial Fumes

The body carries memories for years of things you've done to it. In smoking, for instance, the blood vessels and the lungs may be tense in memory of having to avoid those poisonous chemicals. There may also be a residue in the lungs. This could also be true to people who breathe in poisonous chemicals regularly in their line of work. There are two ways of clearing them out, physical and mental, and both are essential.

For the physical cleansing, sit still, and when you inhale, force your stomach and chest to expand to their utmost. Then very slowly exhale, forcing the chest and stomach to contract to their utmost. Do this for even as little as half-a-minute. This is to change the consciousness of the lungs to know that the damaging chemical is no longer coming in, that they can relax. Lungs have an almost sexual desire to open up and take in as much air as possible. When the smoke comes in, though, they contract in resistance, in avoidance. They stay contracted in fear, even after you've stopped smoking, no matter how long ago, because of this memory.

The other healing is mental, using visualization. Imagine that when you inhale, you're taking in a soft, blue, healing vapor that comes in and soothes your lungs. As you exhale, imagine that the blue vapor is pushing out the dirt and residue. Again, you need do this only half-a-minute or so a day for a while. What it does is to stimulate the unconscious parts of the brain to get to work on healing your lungs.

The Habit Transforming Diagram for Tobacco

In each chapter, we will be reproducing a diagram, which is like a mandala for the abuser of a particular substance. Habits get programmed into the brain, just as circuits get programmed into its mechanical equivalent, the computer. These diagrams are meant to reprogram the brain circuits which perpetuate the habit, and in addition, they achieve some of what the substance is meant to achieve for the abuser. On the following page is the diagram for smokers. Do it several times a day, especially on waking and before going to sleep, in order to help with the dream changes smoking tries, but fails, to achieve. Focus on the vertical parallel lines in the center of the diagram. Force your eyes to go up the line to the dot five times without stopping. You may wish to xerox this and carry a copy with you to work with when you feel the urge for a cigarette. If you're more oriented to movement and touch than to vision, you may wish to redraw the lines, in the air or on paper, each time you use it.

The Right Use of Tobacco

Native Americans were intensely aware of the right use of tobacco. It was seen as a holy gift from the spirit world, and the ritual smoking of it, the passing of a pipe from one group member to another, was a form of holy communion. It induced feelings of peacefulness and wholeness and a balance of individuality and group consciousness in those who shared it. The right frequency of tobacco use is once a week, and the right time to use it is at twilight. It could be used on Friday evening, as a focal demarcation between your regular work week and the different, quieter, more inwardly centered time of the weekend.

Commercial cigarette tobacco is processed, with sugar added. We suggest that you purchase loose tobacco of the purest variety possible, sugar free, and that you either roll your own cigarettes or buy a special pipe to use. Native American shamans say that Bull Durham is the purest commercial blend. This ritual is best performed in an informal group, where you gather in a small circle.

Close your eyes, and visualize a ring of white light surrounding the group. Feel that as you breathe in deeply, you are creating and entering a different time-space. Know that your weekend will be a sort of emotional haven or retreat from the world. Passing around a cigarette or pipe, lightly inhaling it, and sharing it is a way of opening to this other level of being. The tobacco is the power tool that opens the door to it. In the same way, with a single other friend or alone, by creating a ring of light around you and lighting the tobacco, you can rightly use this power tool to change. Once a week, a few puffs, and you enter the change subtly.

There is something in the fire, something in the herb burning, that kindles other feelings in the heart. Fire, smoke, and scent are the three prongs of the key to the door of relaxation and out-of-time peace. For those who wish to have no tobacco enter their system, the same ritual can be conducted by burning herbs, spices, or incense, and passing it in a circle. Burning tobacco can be the intermediate stage between this once a week smoking and the ultimate step of simply burning incense.

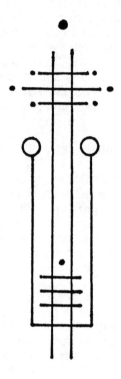

HABIT TRANSFORMING DIAGRAM

FOR TOBACCO

EXERCISE: The Luminous Puffer, a Dream Tool

This exercise is for anyone addicted to cigarettes, or anyone who is having trouble remembering dreams and who would like to do dream work. For smokers, do it whenever you feel the need to light up. Also do it just before you fall asleep, as would those who want to be more aware in dreaming. You may wish to keep pen and pad by your bed in order to write your dreams down in the morning. Allow about two weeks of comfortably doing this before you will see any changes in your dreaming.

Here are the steps:

Put yourself in the bubble of white light.

Feel your bubble surrounded by swirls of the most beautiful and glowing blue-green light. It changes from dark to light, from indigo to aqua to emerald to turquoise, or to any shade to which you feel particularly attuned.

Begin to feel the cloud of light seep into your bubble, bringing along with it a cooling, calming change in your mental state.

Now the light is entering your body. As it pours through your skin, you feel your body changing. It is no longer your physical body that you are feeling, but your body of light, your dream body. With this dream body, you can sink or float or fly or swim through the air. You are lighter than air. You can travel through walls, through space, or time. You are weightless and timeless.

If you're in bed, stay in this state until you drift off into sleep. By moving into sleep in this state, with your mind already altered, you change the patterns of dreaming you have built up over the years. And as you're more aware of the dream state while waking, then while you sleep you will also be more aware of the waking part of your life and will be able to use dreaming more consciously to solve problems.

Techniques for Improving Dream Recall

Dreams are a primary arena for getting back in touch with our visions and working them out. They also serve other functions, like figuring out what to do about our problems and providing a safe outlet for emotions. Being in a deeper level of consciousness while asleep, we're also more open to psychic experiences and to messages from our Core Self. Many addictions, most especially to tobacco and marijuana, stem from difficulty in using the dream place.

If you begin now to pay attention to your dreams, you'll begin healing your addiction, and you'll also have a richer experience of the material in this book as it applies to you personally, since your own capacity for vision will be stimulated. Books on how to work with your dreams will be listed in the bibliography section in the Appendix. Below, however, are some techniques people have found useful in improving their ability to remember dreams.

A firm intention to recall and understand your dreams is the key to remembering them. Each night before you go to sleep, repeat this intention. If you have specific problems in waking life you'd like inspiration about, ask for help with that also.

Keep a note pad or blank book by your bed, and don't jump out of bed when you wake up. Spend a few quiet moments searching for memories of your dreams. Write them down and see what meaning you get from them. Don't worry if they seem jumbled and hard to understand at first. The more you work with them, the clearer they'll get.

If you don't begin remembering dreams right away, don't become discouraged. Keep affirming your intention to remember and work with them.

Reading books about dream interpretation will help increase your confidence and skill in this area. Anyone can do it. Children in the "primitive" South Pacific tribes learn to do this by the age of five, so it isn't really hard.

Essences and Stones to Help with Dream Work

There are also essences and stones to help with dream work. According to Katrina Raphaell, all colors of jade are good dream helpers. (*Crystal Enlightenment*.) We suggest you wear jewelry made of jade. You might even wear it to bed, or you might tape a piece of unset stone on your third eye or keep an item made of jade next to the bed. The essences, in general, work on problem solving within the dream state if taken before bedtime. However, there are several which specifically work on dreams. CALIFORNIA POPPY is related to psychic and creative awakening and to past life information, but much of this benefit is achieved during sleep. CHAPARRAL stimulates emotional cleansing during sleep. ST. JOHN'S WORT helps with troubled dream states and improves the contact with a Higher Power.

Although we haven't worked with the following essences, Gurudas recommends them in his book, *Flower Essences and Vibrational Healing*. He says that CELANDINE produces lucid dreams and increases receptivity to instruction from one's spirit guides; that HARVEST BRODIAEA works on the crown chakra and activates the pituitary gland, thereby increasing the dream state; and that YERBA SANTA opens the doorway to information from the higher self which helps to resolve emotional issues.

Stones to Help with Tobacco

We spoke earlier of stones and their capacity to transmute tobacco and other smoking herbs when we discussed pipes and other containers of smoking substances. You might wish to research various stones used for pipes and discover their meaning and use before selecting one to use in your weekly tobacco ritual. If you haven't been able to let go of tobacco smoking yet, you may wish to use a pipe rather than cigarettes. An incense burner of jade might be an excellent choice for burning tobacco or other herbs and spices.

This is a substitute crystal tool for initiating the same shifts in consciousness that tobacco creates. You'll need a small piece of smoky quartz, about the size of a walnut, and a piece of blue flourite, about the size of a marble. Hold the smoky quartz in your right palm and the flourite in your left. Let their energies wash through you and retune your two brain hemispheres. Do this at those times when you might have turned to a cigarette. Inhale the energy of the stones through your palms deeply. Hold the energy in your chest and feel its power.

Essences to Help with Tobacco

Our guides say that flower essences are especially important as a tool for people who smoke various substances, such as tobacco, pot, or hashish. With pollution, we inhale far too much negativity into our lungs and bodies as it is. Plants which would be toxic to smoke are safe in essence form and aren't addictive. Also, all the useful plants are not available everywhere and at all times, whereas the essences are. The essences partake of the vibrations and energies of the plants in a far less physical way; they work on even subtler, yet far more powerful levels, than the things we could smoke. The time will come, the changed human vehicle will come, when even the essences are not needed. We'll simply tune into the vibrations of the plant, by meditating on it and by contacting the nature spirits directly. But that time is in the future, and essences are here now.

The essences particularly related to tobacco and its function are the following. TOBACCO itself has recently been introduced as an essence, but we have no knowledge of its effects as yet. SAGE is also available as an essence, said to be helpful in stimulating higher states of consciousness and in aligning the mental and spiritual bodies. MALLOW helps with puberty and the crisis of adolescence. QUAKING GRASS, for the blending of egos within a group, to produce group consciousness.

SWEET PEA is also useful for teenagers in the rebellious stage or for others who fail to feel part of society. When the solar plexus is involved, SUNFLOWER is excellent.

CHAPTER FIVE

MARIJUANA AND OTHER ORGANIC DRUGS: A BRIDGE BETWEEN TWO WORLDS

Organic Drugs

The focus of this chapter is on addictive substances derived from naturally occurring products that are subject to minimal processing and treatment. The major substance we'll be dealing with in this chapter is marijuana, which is generally the smoked tops, stems and leaves of the hemp plant. Let's begin by noting that this chapter and the previous one on tobacco are a pair in the same way that the chapters on sugar and alcohol are a pair. The material in the previous chapter on the holy rites and functions of smoking applies equally to marijuana, as do many of the observations about the Sixties generation and their incarnational roots among the Native American people. Since it would be wasteful to repeat all those observations here, we suggest that you read that chapter also.

Hemp is an annual herb originally from Asia and is now widely cultivated all over the planet because of its many uses. Hemp fiber is used in making cord, paper, and cloth. The seeds are used as bird food, and the oil from the seeds is used in manufacturing paints, varnishes, and soaps. Marijuana was long considered a healing herb, and is used today to reduce the negative side effects of chemotherapy and in the treatment of glaucoma. Hashish, another hemp product, is made from the dried resins found on the surface of the female plant and is more potent than marijuana but used less frequently in the West.

Several other substances fall into this same category, and we mention them, although they are less frequently addictive. Peyote is a cactus that grows in the southwestern United States and in Mexico. The drug peyote is produced from its tubercles. It's a hallucinogen that produces visions and changes in perception. Peyote has been used for thousands of years for trance work by native shamans, and is used today as a sacramental substance by the Native American Church, which blends Christianity with Native American, largly Navaho, beliefs. The active ingredient in peyote is mescaline.

Several varieties of mushroom produce substances that are also found in this category. They have been used in every part of this planet by human beings wanting to induce altered states of consciousness. They are seldom addictive, but serve the same consciousness-altering function as do other substances in this category.

Why Marijuana and Hashish are a Mid-Eastern Power Tool

Alcohol has been the main addictive substance of the West. The Christian west and the Jewish world saw wine as a sacramental beverage. But in Moslem countries alcohol was forbidden, and marijuana and hashish were frequently used as power tools. On a collective level we might say that the lesson of the West and the Middle East were not the same. Alcohol, the tool of the West was designed to open the heart and further heart-connected awareness. Wine works on the heart chakra, thus doing some of the things Christianity strove, however vainly, to do for its followers. Of course, misuse of that substance ultimately prevents heart opening from happening.

In Asia and the Middle East, that part of the West that bridges East and West, the lessons that needed to be learned were not the same. Different kinds of visions were required that fostered the use of different power tools. Mohammed forbade alcohol in the Moslem countries, because he felt it was getting in the way of the Arab countries empowering themselves. It may have also come out of his rejection of the Judeo-Christian mystical rites involving wine. There was also a shift in chakra emphasis marked by this religion. Mohammed was a soldier and not interested in opening up the heart chakra. His interest was the root chakra, and also the integration and building of bridges between various chakras, which is what marijuana does.

In the Sixties, marijuana became widely used in mainstream America, at times as an alternate to alcohol and at times as a complement. It's no accident that in the Sixties as the youth of the West began to reject Western values and turn to the East, a tool of the Middle East would become popular, to help us build new bridges in our consciousness.

Organic Drugs and the Wish to Open Up Vision

Sitting in their caves or cloisters, the great hermits of all times have reached deep into the source of vision and opened up light fountains from which others could drink. When one is afraid to make this journey, organic drugs can aid in opening the doorway. Initially they make the body so like air that it can enter the dream state. Yet, with abuse, they so cloud and obscure the dream place that no visioning can happen, and they so weaken the body that it cannot look outward anyway. In a world such as ours, the potential shaman or sybil keeps on using the power tools for vision over and over, but the tools are no more than a key to a door that our culture will not allow to be opened.

The Bowery bum and the junkie have access to these worlds. Lest we romanticize or elevate them, however, they aren't the only ones to have such access. Everyone has access. Some are afraid, some do not look at all. Bowery bums and junkies, in reaching out for these power tools, are at least grappling with questions that the smug, complacent, or self-zombified are denying altogether. It is easier to laugh at someone who trips and falls than to laugh at someone who never gets out of his or her seat at all.

At a time like this, the appeal of consciousness-altering drugs is strong, as a tool for sustaining vision if it seems to be drying up. Or, as an external validation for vision in a culture that acknowledges the power of mushrooms more than the power of meditation. Tools like LSD have a function and are similar to organic drugs used the world around to deepen insight. But whereas in traditional cultures, they are used as part of a movement away from ego, here they are often used in rebellion, in ego affirmation. So they give a glimpse of vision, but without internal work, they ultimately carry one away from it. The inner energy that should rightly go into changing our society gets trapped in the power of the drug itself.

Marijuana as a Power Tool

Much of what was said in the chapter on tobacco, about the ancient holy origins and purposes of smoking, applies to marijuana as well—so you may wish to read that if you have not. Marijuana is used by people who have difficulty standing in the doorway between the dream place and the waking place. People who are afraid of one or the other, or of one flowing into the other instinctively turn to marijuana because of its healing ability in opening these doorways. If you're afraid of the dream place, the inner smoke of marijuana helps it slowly drift into your waking world. If you're afraid of waking—if you'd like to stay in the dream place all the time—marijuana helps with that balancing. Often, for instance, people who are beginning to receive psychic information or teaching in their dreams but who are afraid to bring it through to their waking consciousness will reach out for this drug. In the section on tobacco, there are helpful tools for working with dreams.

The danger of marijuana comes from its strength. With limited usage, you can open that doorway between the two places and learn to turn from one to the other freely. Repeated use of pot sets you spinning like a top in the doorway so that you never enter either place fully. In the dizziness of your turning, you lose the ability to tell which is which. Dream looks like waking, waking looks like dream. Each becomes more clear for a moment, then you spin faster and faster, and all becomes only a gray blur, as you get caught in a revolving door.

We learn through dualities, weaving information between different places. When we blur the distinctions between the two great places, dream and waking, the mind will need to create a new duality. A second addiction is often used to do this, so it is not unusual to go from pot addiction to alcohol, harder drugs, or sugar. Another way of creating the needed duality is to go into a massive illusion, like living in a fantasy world or living in profound anxiety or despair.

Finally, instead of weaving between dream and waking, you weave between gray blur and fantasy. You lose your grounding in the waking world, you turn and turn, you see endless sorts of pictures, but you never MOVE anywhere. Conscious work with dreams and with bringing them into your waking world and utilizing them can help you. The suggestions given in the chapter about tobacco can help you, as can the books about dream work listed in the bibliography.

Pot and the Chakras

When you smoke pot, it seems like it's doing things to your third eye, but it's also doing things to the root chakra. In a sense, these two chakras are the two worlds that marijuana bridges, root being waking/world consciousness and third eye being dream/other world awareness. We hold in common with all animal life on this planet that our root chakras are strongly connected to the planet. An energy shift in the root chakra is the first step toward shifting away from rootedness in this reality and on this world. Pot acts as a root chakra energy rephaser. Thus pot has a particular appeal to the rootless and alienated, who yearn to make a change in their rootedness. Yet, by abusing marijuana, they make it harder and harder to do the work of establishing new roots.

It's no accident that pot became popular again in the Sixties, when everyone felt uprooted from the past, family, and culture. Something in the collective unconscious knew that pot had something to do with shifting energy in the root chakra. People who tried it felt, however subliminally, energy moving in that center. The irony is that the energy shift was actually AWAY FROM, rather than towards greater rootedness, greater alienation being the consequence. Not all of us smoked it, but a large percentage tried it just once or twice, and that exposure was enough so that all our roots shifted. Yes, it's necessary that we uproot from the planet in order to go off-world, but it happened far too early, and there has been much unhappiness as a result. Marijuana does have the capacity to awaken the third eye's sense of expanded vision, but unrooted vision is of little use to anyone still living in a body.

We saw earlier that cigarettes are related to puberty, but marijuana is more related to the young adult of today. We remember that at that age we are supposed to have our roots already—family, home, career, all established—but in this more complex world, young adults are often still in college or graduate school or serving some sort of apprenticeship. Thus they get drawn to this root chakra shifting tool as an expression of their puzzlement and frustration that the rootedness they need is not happening.

Using light to cleanse the root chakra, as in the exercises in Chapter One, is very important. You may also wish to nourish the root chakra by visualizing yourself drawing green or amber light up from the earth into the root chakra through the tailbone. Sit on the floor to do this, or best of all, on the ground. Declare that this is home, that you accept this as your home.

The parts of the physical body most effected by pot smoking are the throat and lungs, and there is an easy secondary contamination of the energy body in the area of the throat chakra. With heavy use of marijuana, there is almost always a residue in the throat center, amounting to a near paralysis of energy there. On a physical level, yes, there can be sore throats, a rasping, but that is nothing compared to its damage to the energy body. Often you are afraid to speak of what you see in that doorway between waking and dreaming; afraid of channeling the vision. Some marijuana addicts have had a past life experience of being beheading or hanged for speaking out, especially about beliefs that were considered heretical in their time.

Just below the throat center is the thymus center, which is the next to be affected as the use of pot continues. Professionals in the field of addiction have spoken of pot addiction as bringing about the "AMOTIVATIONAL SYNDROME." Although few such professionals recognize the chakras, they do perceive the effects on the thymus, for all amotivational means in plain language is that the individual has less and less will to do anything. Be sure to repair and clear out these two centers, the throat and thymus, in order not to be drawn back, subtly into the addiction. Or, even if you don't go back, if the damage goes unrepaired, energy is blocked, and nothing gets accomplished.

The Habit-Transforming Diagram for Pot

In each chapter, we'll be reproducing a diagram which is intended to reprogram brain circuits which perpetuate the habit of abusing a particular substance. On the following page is the one for marijuana. It will help you get out of the archway, help you learn to make clearer distinctions between dream and waking. Thus, it's especially important to use it just before

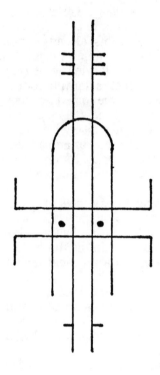

HABIT TRANSFORMING DIAGRAM

FOR MARIJUANA

you go to sleep and soon after waking. Use it several times in the day and especially at any point when you are feeling the need for a joint. Focus on it, and run your eyes back and forth between the two parallel vertical lines without being distracted by anything.

The Right use of Marijuana

As we've said, marijuana is a sort of bridge between worlds. It's mild enough to open consciousness changes without being excessively damaging to the body. But as with all power tools, there is a right and wrong way to use it. Smoking more than once-a-week and smoking beyond the point of first noticing changes in awareness are wrong uses of this tool. Marijuana, when rightly used, provides a bridge between two places. Wrongly used, it transforms the user into the bridge itself, but melts away the two places it should join. A bridge in space is of little use, don't you agree?

As we discussed under tobacco, the smoking of pot and other consciousness-altering substances was once a ceremonial rite engaged in by the tribe. It was done in the safety of a group of related or root-joined people who had a long history together. This condition in itself was protection against the alienation that root-chakra shifting can bring about. Maybe they shifted, but they all shifted together.

The right use of marijuana is at the very most once-a-week joining with others in a quiet circle to pass a single joint and share in the changes, often with music to focus on. A suggested time to use it would be at the end of your weekend or at the end of a vacation, when the quiet, slower energy of relaxation must give way to the faster pace of being at work or in school again. In these situations, pot can provide a bridge for carrying some of your relaxation back into your work week with you. Obviously, if you have been severely addicted to pot, and any exposure to it triggers your addiction, this option may be closed to you.

The Right Use of Other Organic Drugs

Organic drugs such as peyote have been used the world over since time immemorial as a stimulant to vision by healers, visionaries, and spiritual seekers. Most would say that the vision gained by drug use is not the same in depth as the vision gained by meditation. We would agree, for in meditation the practice and slowness weaves the vision into the person in a way that no drug can.

However, as the seasons change, as the year shifts into winter, and the fullness of spring and summer recedes, you might want to go on a vision quest for something to carry you through the cold times, a vision for you to work on in the days of semi-hibernation so conducive to thought and practice. This once-a-year time can be a good one for using a naturally-occurring drug to open your vision.

Do this in a group. Do this with people you trust in the very center of your being. Sit in a circle holding hands. Put yourself, each of you, in your bubble of white light. Then surround your circle of friends with a neon tube of gold light, to carry in warmth through the winter. Chant together any chants that appeal to you, known or spontaneously created. Partake of the drug, ingesting or smoking it. Draw the power of the earth that lies in the drug into your body, feeling the power of vision rise up in you. Pull that power down into your solar plexus, and store it there for the winter. End your ritual by chanting and sharing your visions. Frequently, in group rituals, the visions of each individual are but a part of the whole, greater vision.

EXERCISE: The Silver Arch Between Worlds; A Substitute for Organic Drugs

Follow these steps:

Put yourself in the white bubble. When you look up above, you will see a large archway of pure silver light shimmering over your head. This is the archway between worlds, for marijuana addicts are those who seek to move better between the two places, but have not learned the way.

On one side of the arch you can see the world you live in clearly, bathed in a soft white light that seems to bring out all the details you do not ordinarily see, the finer points, the subtler places that you miss because you are half in a dream.

As you turn around in the span of the archway, you will be looking out into the dream world. It's very like the world you live in, but this world is bathed in a soft blue light. Notice the details here, how the same chair you usually sit in, when bathed in blue, has the mysterious capacity to seem almost alive. It would not surprise you to see it get up and walk away, although at this moment it's resting.

Stand peacefully in the arch, looking now one way, now the other. Keep turning beneath the arch, feeling yourself to be a citizen of both worlds, ready and about to step off capably into either of them—the same world, bathed in two different lights.

When you feel comfortable about being in this place, shrink the silver arch down until it rests like a band over the top of your head from ear to ear.

Then drop it down further, so it rests inside your brain, linking the two halves of it.

Dissolve your bubble, knowing that you are working on linking these two worlds more and more each time you do the exercise, strengthening your ability to be whole in both of them.

Essences and Stones to Repair the Damage Done by Pot

Of the flower essences, a number are helpful for marijuana and its effects on the root chakra. CORN is especially relevant, with the capacity to help balance between spiritual and earthly roots. SQUASH and MANZANITA are also good for grounding and being at home in the body. SHOOTING STAR helps reestablish the feeling of being at home on the earth. WALNUT is a balm for people who feel uprooted, whether due to marijuana or moving, and especially helps those in transitional states.

CLEMATIS is good for the kind of dreaminess and spaciness that pot and other addictions bring. Among the gem essences, OPAL is for clarity, especially for those coming off addictions. FORGET-ME-NOT helps with clarity of thought and disturbed sleep. NASTURTIUM is good for people who live in their head. ST. JOHN'S WORT helps with troubled dream states and enables people to trust their Core Self and the Divine enough to feel at home with visionary experiences.

As for stones, green tourmaline, carnelian, pyrite, and hematite are excellent to wear for feeling grounded and rooted in this reality. Smoky quartz is another stone which is wonderful for grounding and which works strongly on healing the root center. It helps you manifest your visions here on earth. Having a worry stone, a plain old rock in a button shape, that you fondle as you think about your problems, is an excellent subconscious reminder that you live here on this planet and have for almost as long as it took that rock to form, so you'd better learn to live with it.

Soil itself begins as stone and has a healing effect on the root chakra. Having some dirt from your ancestral home, maybe kept in a jar to run your fingers through, is a nice way of making connection with your roots. If dirt from your home turf is unavailable, then dirt from the ground around where you live now is also helpful—and maybe even more useful. Burying your feet in the earth or sand and drawing energy from the earth up through them is restorative.

There's also a crystal substitute for pot and other natural vision-seeking drugs. You'll need a small chunk of carnelian and a piece of azurite about the same size or a little smaller. Hold the azurite in your left hand and the carnelian in your right. Feel the pulsations of energy emanating from the two stones and let it spread throughout your body, merging and filling it with power. Feel that you can hold this energy in your chest and move out from it. You can also carry these stones with you, if you have two pockets and put the stones on their proper side.

CHAPTER SIX

THE ILLUSION OF SUGAR AS LOVE

Sugar IS a Drug

Some of the things we say in this chapter will be hard to swallow. Sugar abusers don't like to think of themselves as addicts. Sure, maybe they eat too much sugar, but that's just because they love the taste of sweets. Sugar IS a drug, and maybe it doesn't alter your consciousness in as immediate and obvious a way as alcohol or pills, but it does produce changes in the physical, emotional, mental, and spiritual state of the user. As an addiction, it's devastating on all four of those levels.

It is in the nature of all addictions to deny that there is an addiction. It is in the nature of all addicts to point their fingers at other addicts and say, "My problem isn't as serious as his." Sugar addicts, in particular, suffer from this form of denial, partly because there's so much denial in our society of sugar's power as a drug. Advertising pushes it on us, social situations push it on us, the giant food producing corporations push it on us. The denial also comes from the fact that, as we'll see later, sugar causes turbulance in the solar plexus, the seat of self-esteem. In order to relieve the resulting self-hate, sugar addicts engage in self-righteousness about the addiction. Keep an open mind about whether or not you are an addict. Keep an open mind about the things we say here. Parts of it will register and work on your higher consciousness, no matter how vehemently you reject it consciously.

What Sugar is, What it Does

Most of our sugar comes from the sugar cane plant, a tall, tropical perennial of the grass family native to Asia. About a third of the sugar we consume comes from the sugar beet or from corn solids and corn syrup. All of these are extracted from the plant, in a chemical process, to give us refined sugar.

Honey and maple syrup are less refined and have more micronutrients than refined sugar, which help the body absorb and metabolize them better.

Molasses, the by-product of refined sugar, contains many of these nutrients also. However, they're just as addictive because chemically they're still the same substance, and they have very similar effects on the energy body. It's important to know that if you're eating ten brownies a day from the finest health food ingredients, you're still a sugar addict.

Starches are closely related to sugar metabolically—as is alcohol—so it's possible to be addicted to starches as well. Starches are carbohydrates, and all carbohydrates are broken down by the body into glucose and other kinds of sugars. There are desperately poor black people in the south who eat boxes of laundry starch in a pure form of the addiction to starch. People who mainly overeat on starch might pride themselves on not being sugar addicts, but that's like people who drink several quarts of beer a day and boast that they never touch the hard stuff.

For the sake of brevity, we'll mainly speak of sugar in this chapter, but if starch is your drug of choice, we mean that too whenever sugar is mentioned. We should also note that this chapter and the one on alcohol are a pair, since they are closely related both chemically and in their effects on the energy body. However, they do not affect consciousness in exactly the same way. (In the same way, the chapters on tobacco and marijuana are related.)

Like alcohol and barbiturates, sugar and starch are in the category of downers or depressants, in terms of their effects on the body, even though sugar acts initially as an energizer or stimulant. Thus, overeating on either causes depression, yet we often overeat when we are depressed, so it can become a self-reinforcing pattern. Long addiction to sugar can damage not only the heart but the liver and pancreas. With a damaged or overactive pancreas, hypoglycemia can result, along with a roller coaster of emotional ups and downs. When the blood sugar level drops low, so does the mood, and more sugar is often consumed to boost it up again. These emotional upheavals can continue for a while after stopping the addiction, until the functioning of the pancreas is normalized. One theory of causation is that an allergy to a substance such as sugar, starch, or alcohol can cause a craving for it that leads to addiction. One route to cure is healing the allergy or avoiding the substance to which you're allergic altogether.

It's important to mention that this chapter is mainly about sugar addiction rather than weight, even though we tend to equate them. It's very difficult to separate the two. Yet, there are overweight people who consume a variety of foods to excess rather than concentrating on sugar and starch, and there are thin people who eat nothing but sugar and who are crazed by it.

Seasonal And Ritual Uses Of Sugar In Our Past

Out of necessity, our eating used to follow a cyclical pattern and consisted mainly of food which was in season at that time and which had been grown in that place. We never used to have desserts every night of the week. Like alcohol, they used to be limited to special occasions— holidays, feasts, and celebrations. They were tribal and family cele- brations, a solidifying of group ties. For many cultures, the only time sweets were eaten were at marriage celebrations, and as we'll see later, this unconscious memory still may influence us in our choice of sugar as a heart-affecting addiction. At the harvest, we had great feasts in which everyone drank, ate, danced, and loved to excess. Now the tribal and family connections are breaking down, and we try to recapture those rapturous occasions by eating sugar all the time.

In winter, we ate more sparsely of the items we could preserve, dry, store, or hunt, and we didn't do so much physical work, but spent more time in quiet craftsmanship or rest. Over the eons, the body adapted to this rhythm, which was the same as the earth's. Today we have the technology to work uninterrupted all year around and to eat whatever we want whenever we want, even if it comes from halfway around the world. Delicious as this may be, the body's eating rhythm and balance of work and rest has been broken, and we no longer communicate with our bodies about what they need.

In many cultures and religions, food was shared in ritual situations. Food was a declaration of friendship, a stranger who ate with you came under your protection. The ritual of communion in many religions af- firmed the soul connection that came when people broke bread together. Today eating together is still a major social pursuit, but often the com- munion is lacking, the heart connection is lacking, and we overeat to fill the void.

Food As A Power Tool

Food also has its uses as a power tool. Native Americans and others ate the flesh of an animal like a wolf or bear ritually to gain the strength, courage, and cunning of that animal. Likewise communion rituals, all the way from primitive times to those in the church today, are a survival of that kind of magic taking in the flesh and blood of Jesus is supposed to give you his holiness. Cannibalism was actually a religious ritual in which eating the flesh of the enemy was supposed to impart his strength.

Today, we all still dimly remember food as magical and use it as a power tool. A person who is ill or upset is urged, "Eat—it will give you strength," even though fasting may actually be better for the body in such situations. Thus, we're programmed from childhood to look to food as a source of strength, and the more strength we need to fulfill our vision, the more we eat in search of it.

The fuel of our bodies is glucose, our primary and most direct power tool. So abuse of sucrose, which is closely related, is partly about fuel, and our foods and are largely devoid of energy today due to all the processing. We confuse food with energy, eating when we're drained. After all, the commercials praise sugar as an instant energy source. Yet if food and energy were the same, the more we ate, the more energy we'd have. Instead, consistent overeating causes a breakdown of the energy body. Processed foods have lost their life force energy, yet we still have the expectation that food will contain it. You may wish to hold your hands over your food and envision white light or energy going into it to revitalize food once more with the life force energy, so you can eat less and be more satisfied.

One of the ways food is powerful is that it seems to be an exceptionally porous medium, readily taking on the energies and emotions of people who handle it. Cookies baked by grandma do carry her love, and we keep on looking for that love in cookies and sweets throughout our lives. One of the authors was given a piece of wedding cake days after the reception and for hours was filled with the joy of the people who were there, even though she didn't know them. It was nothing like a sugar high; it was the kind of ecstasy people are looking for in sugar or other drugs.

Unhappiness and alienation can be imprinted into food, too, by those who are unwilling but powerless members of the food chain. Resentful, lonely housewives imprint their frustration into the food they prepare, and many housewives are unhappy today at their role. Meat carries with it the terror of the animals in the slaughter house. One reason sugar is so devastating is that it's saturated with the bitterness of the sugar cane workers, whose working conditions are not so far removed from slavery. All their unhappy feelings go into the sugar as they grow and process it— all their resentment, all their pain, all their feelings of powerlessness. As you take in the food, you also take in the unhappiness, resentment, and alienation—feelings food addicts have in abundance. Sugar is such a poisonous substance that even touching it can poison your consciousness.

More and more commonly, our food is grown and prepared by the disenfranchised and powerless—food processing and restaurant workers are the lowest on the wage scale, housewives get no respect—so it's not surprising that we feel less and less of the love we are looking for in food and more and more powerlessness over it. Food was a different matter when it carried only the energies of family members who grew and prepared it.

Size, Class, and Power

Although this is primarily a chapter about the addictive substance, sugar, rather than about obesity, there are also some ways in which the matter of size enters into the picture. Ages ago, in earlier stages of evolution of the human vehicle, you had to be large in order to contain as much of the spiritual energies as was needed to be in touch with guides or to do healing. Women learned first on this planet to tune in to these energies, so there were huge women priestess and healers who brought these kinds of energies and spiritually inspired wisdom to their tribes. Because the human vehicle has evolved and so have discarnate beings, it's no longer necessary to ground these energies in largeness. Yet we have a dim race memory of that time and unconsciously tend to equate growth in size with spiritual growth. Thus many of us, especially women, who are opening up psychically have a concurrent weight gain. Many psychotherapists and other healers also struggle with weight and with sugar.

Another reason why priestesses, sybils, or shamans of all eras including our own have struggled with addictions to sugar or its near cousin, alcohol, is because of their effects on the heart center, which we'll learn more about presently. People with these abilities are now and ever were in a peculiar relationship to the group. They are held in awe, but not in love. Excesses of eating or drinking are undertaken to make up for the isolation of being in that position.

From spiritual power being equated with largeness, we next moved to equating size with secular power. This began because for many ancient cultures, spiritual power was attributed to those in secular power—the god/kings and priest/chieftans. As rulers and other high officials became more and more secular, they still clung to largeness as an indication of power. Wealth, power, and largeness became linked together, and in truth only the wealthy could afford to overeat in survival-oriented regions and eras. Thus there's also an unconscious equation of size and wealth. Today the affluent shun and disdain largeness, and yet the poor and the upwardly mobile from working class origins, being closer to the survival level, may still make that subconscious equation.

Today people who are poor and people who come from a peasant heritage tend to have more serious struggles with overweight. There's apparently an inherited tendency to have more fat cells in the body, cells which cry out to be filled because they dimly remember or are sympathetically affected by the threat of starvation their ancestors faced. The body has a powerful memory, more strongly imprinted than the brain. Given the survival of the fittest, people whose bodies carried more fat cells had more capacity to live and to reproduce.

The problem of serious obesity is primarily a female one. This has much to do with the women's lack of power and with their relationships to men. We all subconsciously remember the matriarchy, and memories of abuses of power during that era are slowly beginning to surface as we wrestle with the issue of power between men and women. They are surfacing now in order for us to deal with them consciously rather than with the unconscious hatred and subjugation of women that men have employed to deal with that legacy up to now. It would be wonderful to be able to say women were always gentle, wonderful, peaceful creatures, but the memories that are beginning to surface in New Age circles challenge that notion.

For our collective evolution, we need to accomplish a balance of power between men and women, and the slow progress toward that balance is beginning now. The conflict and tension between men and women, however, may get worse before they get better, as the issue gets more conscious. Men cruelly, almost forcefully, reject large women because of subconscious memories of the era of the matriarchy and that just following, when largeness was needed in order to ground spiritual power. Men subconsciously want women to be smaller in order to more readily dominate them.

Women with serious weight problems are often those who are grappling with the issue of knowing and using their power. Perhaps in various incarnational periods, they suffered consequences for attuning to spiritual power—such as in the eras of religious persecution of witches. The equation of wealth, size and power also comes into it. Studies show that women are poorer than men and that the poorer you are, the more likely you are to be seriously obese. Women need to recognize that they can have power without size. Getting the memory that largeness once contained and represented power can help. Getting the memory that we've all been both men and women hundreds of times in our incarnational history can help. Dependency on sugar or any other substance is now outmoded in our evolution, just as it's outmoded to be overweight, but we all need training in how to be powerful on the subtle body level in order to be free at last of addiction.

The Industrial Revolution and the Growth of Food Addictions

Although sugar grows naturally on this planet, it's only since the industrial revolution that the world-wide consumption of sugar has multiplied so dramatically. Human beings have always had a love of sweets, and honey, maple syrup, and other sweeteners have always been used when available. But as everything strives for balance, the deadening of feeling created in an industrial world required a tool to open and stimulate the heart. Sugar is the simplest, most readily available one, but not necessarily the best one. It's a simple power tool and seems to do the job of opening the heart, but its corrosive powers ultimately undo the very work it set out to accomplish. This is the message that comes from all substances used as power tools. So the individual and collective movement toward sugar indicates right intentionality and a poor sense of direction.

Our eating patterns have changed vastly over the last century. For example, our consumption of sugar has increased from 12 pounds a year per person in 1810 to over 128 pounds now. There are also vast changes in family eating patterns—we now eat over half of our meals away from home, and those we do eat together are often in staggered shifts or in front of the t.v., electronic stimulation taking the place of a family exchange of heart energy. We'll find later that the only safe place to consume sugar is with a group of people we feel lovingly connected to—yet these changed patterns mean family connections are no longer so easy to come by. The food is devoid of the very energy and strength we're looking for, not only on the nutritional level, but also in life force energy and love, since it's prepared by machines or unhappy strangers, rather than with the love and concentration of a family member.

Other things have changed, too, such as the disappearance of breast feeding, which not only gave the child a solid physical foundation and certain natural immunities, but also a foundation of energy body and chakra development, due to receiving energy from the mother's energy field and heart chakra. It was replaced by a formula containing sugar, so the equation of sugar with love is learned very early. Although breast feeding is making a resurgence, those of us who are old enough to be addicts may well have been affected by this physical and energy body deficit. Certain formulas, such as the condensed milk and Karo syrup so common in a particular era, may also have conditioned us to want sweetness and to raise our children the same way.

World War II was a pivotal point in the development of our collective abuse of sugar. It opened us to the possibility of planetary destruction. Renewed prosperity came with it, the end of the terrible depression years, but along with the prosperity came this terrible emptiness of con- templating extinction. We wanted to simulate a joy and a prosperity that we didn't really feel. The emptier we felt, the more we needed the trappings of celebration. There's also a matter of class-consciousness involved. For most of history, only the rich could afford to have sugar. Now with prosperity, we felt we should eat it all the time. Every time we have sugar, we support the cultural lie that everything is fine, that there is endless prosperity, and that everyone is happy. Children are given candy, cookies, and snacks to cover up the emotional barrenness of life, the lack of true vitality.

At the same time that sugar is becoming a major contaminant of our foods, thinness is becoming the Twentieth Century fetish. We'll see in various chapters that addictions wax and wane in popularity in response to the decisions, conditions, and needs of the human collective. Thin came in during the 1920's as the direct result of the growth of advertising.

Increasingly we compare ourselves to media idols and hate ourselves when we don't measure up. Yet society and that same media give us double messages, pushing food on us and putting sugar in everything, then selling us diet foods and books. Anorexia is the logical end-product of the thinness fetish. This disease primarily strikes teenagers, and a study by Yale University shows that 46% of teenage girls think they are fat, while by standard measurements only 7% actually are. Some women are also addicted to dieting, with its starvation-induced highs and lows.

As other addictions become less and less socially acceptable—smoking in public, being intoxicated—we can become more and more addicted to sugar. At the same time, however, we've made a collective choice to perfect the body, so we're obsessed with thinness and fitness, and it becomes less and less acceptable to be overweight. These two schizophrenic sets of demands set up very destructive coping mechanisms—binge vomiting, the alternation of stuffing and starving, and the use of artificial sweeteners, which we'll discuss later.

The Heart Chakra—Sugar Addicts As Love Addicts

The primary addiction sugar addicts have is to love, yet the heart chakra break-down of our culture, with all the losses and alienation, means that many of us experience very little love in our daily lives. One reason the confusion between sugar and love arises is that sugar brings a rush of blood to the heart, so we think the heart chakra is being nourished. The very words we use to charm our lovers show this connection—sweetie, sweetheart, sugar, honey. Ultimately, what sugar does is to weaken the walls of the heart and blood vessels so that more and more sugar has to be used to create the same rush. Instead of taking in sugar to get love rushes, the sugar addict can nourish the heart chakra through the exercises in Chapter One.

It would be nice to say that everything evolves into higher and higher states of consciousness, but some things devolve in a parallel and opposite direction; because free will is an element of every level of reality. Planets choose to move in the same orbit over and over—that's an element of their free will. Order is a free choice that the universe makes, not an imposition on it from the outside. So it would be nice to say that if you choose to eat a lot of sugar your heart would really open. But every free choice isn't necessarily the best one.

Sugar is especially used to manipulate love in children. To be simplistic for a moment, the adults in all young sugar addicts' lives were liars in the matter of love. They simply didn't know how to express love to their children, and they lied about love to themselves and everyone else. Their children grew up believing they were loved, but no love reached their heart center, which shriveled and left them starved for love. Unfortunately much of what we call love is manipulation. We're part of a chain of people—our parents, grandparents, great-grandparents—who were brought up on manipulation and never learned how to love.

Women in traditional roles give their hearts to those they endlessly nurture and don't get much love or recognition for it. They pump heart energy out, but very little comes in. This tempts them into sugar addiction to fill the heart energy void. Then the heart center shuts down from the sugar and from the sadness, and even less heart energy comes in or goes out. The painful feelings of isolation, alienation, and lovelessness which result are difficult to bear, and the networks of support that once existed—family, neighbors, friends—are either breaking down or constantly disrupted in this mobile society of ours. A lasting, committed relationship gets harder and harder to come by. Often sugar is not enough, so women in this bind may be drawn into multiple addictions to ease the pain—cigarettes, coffee, compulsive shopping, maybe even a little valium.

It's very hard for food addicts to let go of sugar without feeling they're letting go of love. Begin with the awareness that sugar is a manipulative tool, a way people have of getting you to love them, of getting you to give them what they don't have. If your grandfather gives you candy and says, "I love you," what he may be saying is, "You'd better love me." People barter sugar for that rush of love out of your heart center. Men give candy during courtship for the same reason. This mechanism isn't so different from alcohol or marijuana offered in a spirit of "fellowship and belonging," drinking buddies, or people who get you drunk or high in order to seduce you. That travesty of love leaves only emptiness in its wake. Your heart center has been ripped off, and you reach out for the chemical to fill up the hole. A puppy or a kitten can teach you more about love than a cookie.

EXERCISE: For Telling the Difference Between Food and Love

If you still tend to equate sugar with love, work with this exercise consistently when temptation arises. One of the powerfully seductive things about sugar is that we all internally know the purity of white light, and sugar is so white. But the whiteness of the sugar is poison, and other poisonous substances are white too—like heroin, cocaine, and refined flour.

Here are the steps you take:

Imagine that you are sitting in a bubble of white light which is just pure love.

Visualize the sugar or other food on the outside of your bubble.

Don't bring it into the bubble, but just at the wall of it, across from your heart. What happens to the light then?

Now put it back outside and get rid of it. Now what happens to the light?

This is the really courageous part of the exercise. Now you've experienced how the substance affects the light, and you've experienced the pure love of the white light. Now picture outside the bubble a person or situation in your present or past where love and belonging were professed. Bring that person or situation up to the bubble and watch what happens. It's a litmus paper for knowing if it's love or not. It's not always clearcut, but sometimes the light will go off altogether.

Other Chakras Affected by Sugar

We spoke in Chapter One about the tendency of a blocked or damaged chakra to spill over into the chakras next door. In this case, the damage done to the heart center by sugar spills over most strongly into the solar plexus. The sugar addict suffers from an agony of self-hate. Yes, it's true that society powerfully reinforces this judgement in its prejudicial and derisive treatment of overweight people. However, in this case, the poisoning of the solar plexus is what initiates the feelings of self-hate, and the sugar addict, seeking to rationalize why the feeling exists, seizes on society's condemnation as the explanation. In addition, when the heart energy is blocked, the person feels unloved, and the resulting solar plexus turbulence gets translated into, "There must be something wrong with me if no one loves me." (There is also some spillover into the thymus center.)

Sugar also has a powerful effect on the root chakra, in that it pulls energy out of it and upward, in the rush of energy toward the heart. There are also secondary effects in terms of the damage modern life has done to the root chakra. We're highly mobile and constantly losing people because we move away or they do. The connections to the extended family are frequently broken. We somehow think that rooted and nurtured are the same, so we're drawn to sweets when we feel unrooted. We sense movement in that chakra from eating sugar, but we fail to realize that the movement is actually away from the chakra rather than toward it. As more and more people suffer uprooting and loss of family ties, we're all more and more drawn to sugar, and we put it in everything. Manufacturers find that sugar sells products, so there's more and more of it in our food.

Root chakra ruptures can predispose you to weight problems, just as they do to alcoholism. (In the companion chapter to this one, on alcohol, we discuss the finding that second generation Americans have more alcoholism than the same ethnic groups did in their own countries.) Root chakra ruptures do not only come from traumatic events in this lifetime, though there is a plenitude of those. They get passed down to subsequent generations in two ways—heredity and incarnation.

Lines of lifetimes at survival level, multiple lives of starvation produce them. As we saw earlier, fat cells get transmitted in the genes, through the survival of the fittest. We posit that the root chakra deficiencies are also inherited, transmitted through generations of parents not knowing how to give root chakra fullness to their children, if nothing else. On another level, those who have had lifetimes of starvation and hardship may carry that memory when they incarnate again. Addictions to sugar and to excesses of food can result.

Fake Sugar, Fake Love

Artificial sweeteners are products of this society's delusion that you can have it all—eat all you want and still stay thin. They stand in the same relationship to real food as credit cards stand to real money. Artificial sweeteners, being synthetic, almost belong in the chapter on synthetic drugs, just as sugar could be included in the category of organically derived but processed drugs like cocaine and heroin. Maybe they don't alter consciousness as profoundly as something like quaaludes, but they damage the energy body, in addition to the damages and alterations to the physical body.

Artificial sweeteners trick the heart center into opening—they're fake love, even more fake than sugar. From sugar, at least you get some kind of high. As time goes on, we're going to find that artificial sweeteners damage the heart even more than sugar or alcohol, because the heart center resents being tricked that way. These substances are already known to cause cancer, and people are becoming aware that they're addictive and can cause depression. The depression is related to the fact that the heart has been cheated into opening, but there's no love energy that rushes into the opening.

We're hooked on artificial sweeteners because of the desperate lack of love in the world today. We get addicted to appearance as a power tool to get others to love us, but "love" based on appearance isn't real, so we crave sugar. But sugar makes us fat, and being fat makes it harder to find love, so fake sweeteners become more appealing.

Desserts and sodas aren't real food, and those sweetened artificially are even less real. They support us in not taking responsibility for what we put in our mouths. So we still don't ask the really fundamental question: Is our food nutritious and does it sustain the life process on the cellular level? If the amount of money invested in promoting, consuming, and researching artificial sweeteners were spent on improving the quality of human life, we wouldn't have so much need for sweeteners—real or artificial. And meanwhile, millions on this planet are starving to death.

EXERCISE: The Sugar Shakes—For Getting Sugar Out of Your System

This exercise is good for when you have sugar in your system, and for long-range cleansing when you've stopped having sugar. In the olden days, they used to prescribe horseback riding when you'd overeaten, because of this same gentle shaking action.

Take these steps:

Remember that sugar is a poison. In order to counteract that, put yourself in a bubble filled with green vapor. Imagine yourself inhaling the vapor deeper and deeper with each breath until your entire body is filled with it. Feel the greenness cleanse and revitalize your system.

Stand up and start to vibrate your arms and legs. Let the vibration spread throughout your body.

Breathing deeply, continue for a minute or two, until you feel cleansed inside.

The Habit Transforming Diagram for Sugar

As we've said in other chapters, behavior and habits are imprinted into our consciousness much the way memory is fed into computers. Addictions create imprints too, and this diagram is designed to clear out and reverse the imprint of the sugar habit on your neural pathways. It will help you to stop and to stay away from the addiction over the long haul. By cleansing and erasing that pattern, you're able to release the energy formerly channeled into your addiction for more constructive purposes. To use the diagram, go into a deep state of consciousness. For several minutes, stare at the circle and nothing else in the picture. Do this at least twice a day for several weeks, or longer if you feel the need. Any time you feel a craving for sweets, do this instead.

EXERCISE: Sweet Light, a Love Tool

Sugar addicts are often looking for love in safe places, free from the threats of human contact. But since sugar is as lethal as any other bad

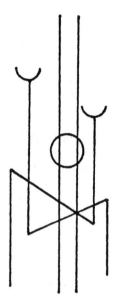

HABIT TRANSFORMING DIAGRAM

FOR SUGAR

relationship, this exercise is planned for those moments when loneliness and despair would drive us to something sugary.

To replace sugar, take these steps:

Sit in your bubble of white light.

As you inhale, imagine that your body is being filled with a soft pink light, entering through your nose and slowly spreading through your entire body, with each breath.

Feel the pinkness gather in your heart. Allow yourself to feel whatever sorrow is impelling you to turn to sugar. Let the pink go to the place where that sorrow is, and cleanse it. Know that the pink has the power to satisfy that need in another form.

Feel the pink on your tongue and know that it is far more healing than any sweet could be.

Affirm your capacity to find love within yourself. Know that when you have done that, you will be in a better place to attract the right love to you from outside, not from a position of need but of wholeness.

When you feel complete with this and know that you have healed another part of your eating habit, then dissolve the bubble and return to your usual consciouness, carrying with you a slow glow of pink light in your heart.

The more often you repeat this exercise, the easier it will be to have the change happen in an instant, anywhere, anytime, anyplace, in a flash, at home, in a cafe, just as you're about to eat something sweet. Work with the pink, as something healthy to do for yourself. We remind you also, if you're still using sugar, that the exercises on stopping your addiction in our earlier book are as helpful for you as for those who use stronger drugs.

The Right Use of Sugar

Sugar is a power tool whose right use is the release of an energy that electrifies the senses and heightens emotional pleasure. The body can only tolerate sugar a maximum of once-a-month. Sugar's vibrations can only be channeled and absorbed when your personal energy is joined by the energies of a loving group of friends, and followed by an activity that will direct and release this stepped-up energy. Dancing is probably the best choice, or a group sing, or a series of relay races, or a game of lawn football. Sugar expands and releases perception. The gift of the right use of sugar is a different, larger, and higher perspective.

It takes the heightened group energy and the release of certain chemicals in the body that happen only at festivals of joy, for the body not to be burned out by the power of sugar. Without a group to recycle the energy, without a group activity to clear it out, any energy released is lost. Hence, depression follows a sugar binge when you sit by yourself over a coke or a pint of ice cream.

To use sugar rightly, once-a-month, at the Full Moon perhaps, gather with friends. Join hands around your sugar-treat and surround yourselves individually and as a group with white light. Then, each of you should direct light into the dessert. Eat it, then dance or sing until you've used the stepped-up energy the sugar gives and moved it out of your system. Even at these gatherings, eat in moderation.

This is a right use of sugar. To avoid a wrong use, eliminate all sugar from your diet. This means checking labels of foods to see if they contain any sugar substance—corn syrup, dextrose, fructose, barley malt, honey, or maple syrup. Sugar is hidden in breads, ketchups, cigarettes, canned fruits, nondairy creamers, cigarettes, cough medicines, and many other unsuspected places. It's popular to believe that honey and maple sugar are healthy replacements for sugar. While they contain certain minerals and nutrients, and while they don't carry along with them the resentment of sugar cane workers, they're still sugar when broken down in the body. If you need to, begin by replacing processed sugar by natural sweeteners, but make it your intention to eventually cleanse your diet of all sweeteners except those consumed at your monthly celebration.

Essences and Stones to Replace Sugar

All the essences given for the heart chakra can help in your healing—especially BLEEDING HEART, TURQUOISE, RUBY, and ROSE QUARTZ. APRICOT and BANANA are both extremely helpful for the hypoglycemia that so often accompanies sugar addiction. POMEGRAN-ATE is excellent for sugar addicts in that it balances emotional extremes due to lack of childhood nurturing. SUGAR BEET and SUGAR CANE are now available as essences, but we have not as yet worked with them.

Refined sugar is in crystalline form, so sugar addicts may especially vibrate to crystals, with clear quartz being especially helpful. However, rose quartz is the primary heart center stone, and we cannot recommend it highly enough. Wear a necklace of its beads, not necessarily expensive, or wear a pendant of this stone on a chain just long enough to cover your heart center. Cleanse the stone frequently in RESCUE REMEDY or ROSE QUARTZ elixer. Sleep with a chunk of it near you, or create in your imagination every night a huge, iridescent egg of rose quartz surrounding your bed, in which you sleep.

This is a substitute crystal tool to use when you're craving sugar or sweets, instead of turning to them. You'll need a piece of rose quartz about the size of a walnut and a piece of clear quartz a little bit smaller. Hold the rose quartz in your left hand and the clear quartz in your right. Cup your hands around them and feel the energy spread through your arms into your chest. Open up to let the energy fill your heart and stomach with warmth and comfort.

CHAPTER SEVEN

ALCOHOL:
A QUEST FOR THE HOLY GRAIL

What many people do not recognize is that alcohol is a drug—one of the more potent and destructive ones when the level of addiction is reached. The fact that it's a liquid dazzles us into thinking it's merely a beverage, perhaps one with euphoric side effects, but still a beverage. Many people who want to cut down on the use of other drugs switch to alcohol, thinking it is less harmful. Although the addiction takes longer and is legal, it's an addiction all the same, and, as we shall see, has powerful effects on the physical, emotional, mental, and spiritual well being of the individual. Far more people die of the effects of alcohol each year than of all other drugs, and alcoholism is ranked within the top four health problems.

Alcohol—or ethanol, ethyl alcohol, or grain alcohol—is the chemical compound found in beer, wine, and liquor. It is produced through the process of fermentation of starches by brewers yeast and other microscopic bacteria. Fermented beverages are found all over the world. Domestication of the vine began around 6000 years ago, and by 1500 B.C, production of wine from crushed grapes and beer from germinating cereals, using malt, was an established technical art in most of the middle east.

Alcohol's Place in Human History

In order to understand alcoholism, we first have to understand alcohol and its purpose and appeal in our lives from the spiritual and emotional perspective. Alcohol has been with us from the earliest settlements. It was not always used in such a destructive way, but was a ritual part of community life. Alcohol and all fermented beverages were introduced centuries ago for the same sort of shift of consciousness as smoking herbs and mushroom, but it was a step forward for the times. Alcohol as a tool was introduced as a concept of our world by disembodied beings. It was designed to alter brain waves beyond the threshold of ordinary occurring primate experiences, and it was joyfully accepted because it did so. It served as a bridge to awaken vision. So we've been chemically manipulated for 10,000 years. Fermented beverages were originally brewed by crones, female shamans, and used in ceremonial rites to awaken vision.

Alcohol and dance go together. Alcohol and loving go together. Alcohol is a tool for release: mental, emotional, physical, or spiritual. The loving we're speaking of here is that which exists in groups, but in the absence of community living, people use it all too frequently as a tool for expression in their personal relationships. But with dance, in large groups of people, at new moons, harvests, and feasts, the alcohol provides a change in energy levels, in that its stepped-up form is channelled by the group energy.

Alcohol originates in grains and fruit. The oldest and most spiritually potent beverage, wine, comes from the grape, which grows in a spiral form, like the turnings of a dance. In those rural settings, people had seasonal relationships to drinking. They planted, tended, and harvested the grapes, crushed them, and stored them until the wine was ready. So the wine had their own energy in it when they drank it at their festivals. While some of it was stored for other uses, mainly for healing, wine was not consumed all year round.

In our culture, there's no room for this tie to the land or this seasonal rhythm of drinking. We live in cities and have so little connection with nature that we've lost touch with the knowledge of how to use alcohol safely. Alcohol and drugs affect us differently at different times of the year, at different phases in the biorhythm of the earth, and thus there are times when it's safer to use them. All foods have this seasonal rhythm, and alcohol is no exception.

People who drink also have a dim subconscious memory that these beverages started out as healing tools. In addition to the ones which have survived, there were many potent medications distilled as spirits which have passed from our memory. Alcohol was the preservative, not the vital ingredient, but we have lost sight of that. Doctors of the recent past and even the present who are fond of prescribing a drink or two for heart patients or to relieve tension are past-life healers who dimly recall that somehow alcohol was part of healing. Doctors who themselves are addicted to alcohol remember it all too well.

Even now, alcoholic beverages have healing herbs in them—although you need not drink alcohol to get the herb. Hops, the main ingredient in beer, is a great healing agent, a natural sedative and digestive aid. Wormwood, the herbal element in vermouth, is an antidote against bitterness and also discharges mucous, but you can brew wormwood as a tea. Both hops and wormwood are available as flower essences. The herbs in alcoholic beverages are no longer potent enough to heal because of the processing. Yet people still turn to alcohol with a collective unconscious memory that these drinks were once used as healers.

It's very easy, however, to romanticize the past, to see the ways that our ancestors were more connected to the earth and its seasons, and to forget the hardship and suffering they lived through. From tribes to city states, it was pretty much the rule that male chieftains and war lords, priests, and kings ruled the people, enforcing rigid social codes with severe penalties for those who disobeyed. It's as if the human global community, moving away from the structure of animal instinct, was not yet ready or evolved enough, (and is barely yet,) to be able to handle human individuality and creativity. The intricate laws of the past sought to duplicate from the outside the old animal order that once came from inner instinct.

But there were always those who saw beyond that rigid structure to the future, who did not fit in, who listened to other gods. And alcohol was one of their power tools. As a whole, societies allowed the use of alcohol on limited occasions as a sort of escape valve. When used, it allowed people to break the bonds that the social order imposed upon them, to shake off the restraints for a day or two. But there were always others who continued to drink, continued to tap into that seemingly anti-social vision, that anarchic vision, that was really a vision of the future of human society.

It's important that we remember that in the west both wine and theater were sacred to the god Dionysus. Plays were used as a tool for expressing the inexpressible, for making those individuals who did not fit in into functional and useful members of the group. By wearing masks, those followers of the god of the vine could say things they wouldn't have been allowed to say without them. In vino, veritas—in wine, there is truth—was a Latin translation of a proverb quoted by Plato in *The Symposium*.

Followers of Dionysus believed that wine was a gift of the gods, a tool for transformation. Alcoholic beverages are even today referred to as spirits, in dim recognition of their ability to open us to the spirit world. What we called gods were actually powerful discarnate guides, elder spirits helping to move human consciousness to new and freer places. But in time the right uses of wine and the shifts in consciousness it brought were forgotten. The rules of how to channel that energy were forgotten or suppressed by the evolving city states and nations. Wine and other alcoholic beverages are still favored power tools for artists and especially writers, but the communal structure that supported them is gone, and the group functions that allowed them to give voice, those feasts and holy days, are gone too.

Drinkers may turn to pubs and bars with a memory of community, but each drinker now turns inward instead. We have come very far from remembering the old, instinctual group patterns our ancestors once knew, but we have not yet evolved patterns that come from the joint celebration of individual egos rather than the merging of them. Alcohol was a tool that took us from one point in our evolution to another. It facilitated our growth from tribal creatures toward our becoming global beings. But alcohol no longer works as a planetary tool. The individuals who use it find themselves trapped like a record with a scratch in it that keeps playing the same words over and over again.

Many individuals who are alcoholics in this life were healers and artists and performers in other lives. It is important for them to honor the capacity for transformation they expressed in the past, without getting hung up on the tool they used then. It's hard to splice apart those two things. But the more alcoholics honor their capacity for transformation, the more they can use the lessons of their addiction to move into new consciousness-altering places, and help move us into the future.

We've come to a point in our history where we threaten the planet itself with destruction. If we're going to survive and continue to evolve, we must reconnect to the planet again without returning to the rigid social codes of the past, and at the same time step into the future without becoming so spaced out that we cannot make practical changes in the world. In different ways, all recovering addicts have within themselves a piece of our future healing. In different ways, we must support that capacity in ourselves and in each other, so we can survive and begin to unfold.

Alcohol and the Collective Search for the Holy Grail

What dreams are to individuals, myths are to the society that creates them. In the west, one of our most potent myths is that of the holy grail, the wine cup Jesus used at the last supper, supposedly a source of endless blessings to anyone who finds it. Wine was used as a sacramental tool in the Middle East long before the time of Jesus, and long before this myth emerged in the Middle Ages. The search for the Holy Grail was one of the major preoccupations of the knights of King Arthur's court. In a sense, all drinkers are looking for their own Holy Grail, their own source of blessing. This quest is part of what gives so much power to our collective alcohol addiction. In a subtle way, it is enshrined in the collective unconscious. Everyone wants to find the holy grail.

An excellent introduction to the grail myth is the book *He* by Robert A. Johnson (Perennial Library, 1977). One of the things it reminds us of in our quest for the grail is that the grail does not exist for personal gratification and reward. The grail is a collective blessing. It's a future blessing. Everyone prospers when it is found. But we have short-circuited our sense of collective healing. We drown in our cups, alone and disconnected from the world. We confuse the contents of the cup with its reward. Ony as we continue to grow and let go of our addictions, can we continue to search for what the grail means instead of what it seems to offer us individually.

The grail is our collective heart. The message of the grail myth to the west is about the necessity of opening the heart. The grail is part of the teaching of alcohol addiction, part of its great healing. Recall again that alcohol powerfully effects the heart center. The quest for the grail is the quest for heart healing. King Arthur's time began the tradition of courtly love and romance, as well as the reintroduction of feminine energy suppressed by the patriarchy of the early church.

Alcohol as a Power Tool

Fermented beverages were made all over the planet to induce altered states of consciousness, for healing rituals, for communication with the spirit realm, as tools to support what we now call channeling, and to open doorways to the world of dreaming. The function of alcohol is to expand consciousness to other levels—as a tool for solving problems in our day-to-day lives. But we've made that shift and alcohol is essentially obsolete, no longer serving us. Alcohol is consciousness nostalgia; all it produces is places people have already been.

Anyone who turns to alcohol remembers this at a deep level. But because our culture denies the reality of the dream world and spirit world, one may go there and have trouble coming back, have trouble making concrete the feelings, visions, and directions that one found there. Then one gets lost in dreams, instead of using the wisdom of dreams to drive their daily life. And one keeps turning back to alcohol, knowing it once had power. But without an anchoring in nature like fermented beverages once gave us, and without an understanding of power tools, alcohol destroys rather than heals. Waking reality becomes as fluid and uncertain as dreams. And dreams become the glamorous lure one constantly swims toward but can never quite reach.

What Your Favorite Drink Reveals About You

The choice of what people drink can be an indication of the kinds of problem solving they are looking for. BEER DRINKERS tend to have excess physical energy they aren't using, which is not being channeled correctly. This is why spectator sports are so often accompanied by beer. When you work all day, energy builds up momentum and beer is a way of leveling that out. Having more than one makes the problem worse by accentuating the energy, aggravating rather than soothing. The key word here is frustration at not having a channel for the energy, and as people have jobs that are less and less physical, beer becomes more and more a national drink. Jogging, aerobics, or other regular exercise can release the bottled-up energy more effectively than a bottle of beer.

WINE DRINKERS have too much mental energy. People who are drinking too much wine should ask themselves, "What mental capacities am I not using well?" Wine drinkers often allow themselves to get caught up in mental labyrinths that go nowhere. Often, their drinking is related to a sadness that as children they weren't allowed to play mentally, so as adults, they overstress mental activities. One small glass of wine, drunk slowly over the course of an hour, will tend to bring energy down from the head and distribute it through the whole body. More than that starts to numb the body and allows the mind to race even more freely. Mental people like writers may sense this and drink too much wine to set the mind racing. This impulse is misguided because in doing so they are losing their grounding.

People who turn to HARD LIQUOR often have problems expressing anger. One small drink—a shot glass—taken slowly over half an hour to forty-five minutes, brings a flush to the body. It can help in the natural release of anger in transmuted ways that are more acceptable than violence, such as loud drinking songs or a cathartic telling of the story of what happened. More than one shot begins to poison the liver, which on a metaphysical level is where anger is processed. Thus the anger doesn't have a proper channel and festers in the liver. The alcohol and the festering anger together ultimately destroy the liver. When you turn to hard liquor, you need to ask yourself what you are angry about.

The key words for the three alcohol addictions—beer, wine, and hard liquor—are frustration, sadness, and anger. These are simplistic divisions, yet can give you a direction to go in your healing. Other people solve these problems in other ways. Almost everyone is frustrated, sad, or angry about some things, but not everyone turns to alcohol as a solution. Some process these problems in the dream state, but others are afraid of their dreams, with their reminders of the life purpose. Small amounts of alcohol bring small amounts of the dream state into waking reality, where you can deal with it more readily. But when you drink too much, you make things even worse because the dream state itself is marred by the drugging. Thus, a "nightcap" which is only that, not the culmination of an evening of drinking, may help with the dream state, but not if needed so regularly that it becomes destructive.

Alcohol's Effects on Your Chakras

Each addictive substance has an initial affinity for one or more of the chakras. Ultimately all the chakras are damaged, but alcohol most strongly affects the heart center. As the heart center gets shut down, energy gets fixated into the lower three chakras, which govern self-esteem, sexuality, and security. The deeper the person goes into alcoholism, the greater the blockage.

As we've said earlier, where there is a chakra blockage, there can be a spill-over effect, so that the solar plexus and the thymus, being next to the heart, can also be affected. Men who drink are often those thrust into positions of too much power, or are often in class and race situations where they are deprived of access to the power they are told they must have to be "real men" in our society. Women who drink are all too often deprived of any access to power at all, which short circuits the energy in us all.

This damage accounts for many of the problems common to alcoholics and those who love them. There is a progressive absorption with the self and withdrawal from contact with the world, a bitter, resentful attitude, and difficulty with sexuality (either promiscuity or impotence). These are all understandable in the light of chakra malfunctioning. It is typical, near the end stages of alcoholism, for the person to experience what is colloquially called "the horrors"—periods of severe and unreasoning anxiety, with terror of the phone, buses, dogs, even the mailbox.

One of the points of this book is that getting sober is not enough. The spiritual malaise which is at the root of the addiction must be dealt with, by finding and working toward the vision or life purpose. The backlog of damage to the energy body must also be healed. All the chakras must be cleansed, most particularly the heart center, which is so strongly affected by alcohol. The heart does not reopen spontaneously, except sometimes in the case of a powerful spiritual awakening or a great love affair. If it remains closed, the person can feel isolated and miserable and thus very vulnerable to relapse. The Many Petalled Flower, given in Chapter One, is particularly effective in freeing the heart center of constriction so that a flow of loving energy is available.

The mates, lovers, and children of alcoholics are also seriously affected by these chakra blockages. On a psychic level, alcoholics and other addicts, even in recovery, have the capacity to siphon off energy from others, yet lack the ability to utilize it. Thus those who live or work with either active or recovering alcoholics often suffer from an energy drain, most especially heart energy—and can develop secondary addictions of their own, such as to sugar, to try to replace the energy. Young children whose parents are heavy drinkers often wind up with malnourished and incompletely developed heart centers of their own. Thus, one of the causes for the high rate of alcoholism among children of alcoholics may be the poor development of various chakras.

In addition to its effects upon the heart center, alcohol consumption also affects the throat and third eye chakras. When the heart center is functioning, it serves as a bridge between the lower and upper chakras. But as the heart shuts down and energy gets stuck in the lower chakras, in order to create a kind of balance, the throat and third eye may open more widely. But with their opening expanded, this situation leads to the delusionary verbosity of addictive individuals, so they can talk the talk but not walk the walk. This creates the patterns of dishonesty and lack of communication so familiar to those who are close to addicts. As the addiction progresses, this imbalance can even contribute to the delirium and hallucinations of the advanced stages. Prohibition taught us that you cannot deal with excess by denial. And the imbalances caused by alcohol tell us that you cannot balance out blocked lower chakras and a shut down heart with two overly opened chakras above.

EXERCISE: The Sea of Gold, An Alcohol Substitute

Alcohol dependency is about the faulty use of energy, and in this exercise we will be working at balance, by going back to the source of so much of the energy in our world...the sun. The following is a meditative exercise designed to help balance your energy field and provide a spiritual alternative power tool to help you do the work your favorite drink did. It works especially well on the heart center.

Here are the steps you take:

Sit in a bubble of pure white light and go down into a deep state of consciousness.

Imagine that you are floating like a jellyfish in the midst of an endless sea of luminous gold liquid light.

Feel yourself breathing in the light as you swim through the water. It enters your bubble, fills it, and then enters your body, reaching every cell and organ, energizing you completely. Let it pour into your heart and fill it, until you feel your heart glowing brightly like an inner sun.

Feel a sense of pure energy inside you. Know that once you have found the way to this place you can return whenever you want. Know that once you have taken in the waters of this place they will change the very way you use energy. Your use of energy will become more efficient, and your ability to use your energy in ways that work for you will increase. You will be changing the magnetic structure of your body, and with that change, you will begin to attract to yourself situations that are right for you. You will find your energy balancing.

When you feel finished with this, dissolve your bubble and return to the usual level of reality. Do this exercise whenever you feel the need for a drink or whenever you want to balance out your energy system, so you can work out the frustration, anger, or sadness.

Habit-Transforming Diagram for Alcohol

One of these diagrams exists for each major addiction. The diagram shown here is designed to clear out and reverse the electrical imprint of the alcohol habit.

To use this diagram, clear your mind of other distractions and sit quietly. Now focus on the diagram. Train your eyes to go up from the two arrows to the circle without stopping. Go up and back to the bottom several times. You may wish to do this exercise three or four times a day at first, until you have a sense that the process is complete.

The Right Use of Alcohol

For many former alcoholics, changes in body metabolism make it impossible for alcohol to ever enter their body again without a negative chemical effect. So if you cannot or don't want to drink wine again, simply remember the grape and how it grows in a spiral pattern whose growth is like the turnings of a dance, and some of the same effect will happen in your brain. Those who feel unable to ingest alcohol might substitute the unfermented grape in this ritual.

Recall what we said earlier, that alcohol and dance go together. Alcohol and loving go together. With dancing, in large groups of people, at new moons, at harvest time and at feasts, the alcohol provides a change in energy level that in its stepped-up form is dealt with and channeled by the power of group energy.

To begin your right use ritual, gather together with friends in a circle. Hold hands and surround yourselves with a ring of bright light. Then pass the wine or beer or whatever you choose in a large cup or goblet, each friend taking a sip. Yes, it is like communion, communion being only the dim racial memory of pre-Christian rites. As you pass it, focus your thoughts on all the things you have to be thankful for. Ground and center yourself in these thoughts. Know that the power of alcohol is such that it can stimulate the release of negativity through dance on a nonconscious level. You don't, therefore, have to be aware of what you want to release. In fact, being aware of it only makes you more attached to it.

Drink from the cup passed around, drink from it three or four times deeply enough to feel yourself buzzing. Then turn up the music and trust the alcohol to do its work of release, for that is what a power tool is—something that aids you in doing the work you have to do—and we all have work to do in releasing negativity. So, drink, dance, and let go. Grounded in thankfulness, in a group, in dance, once a month at the most.

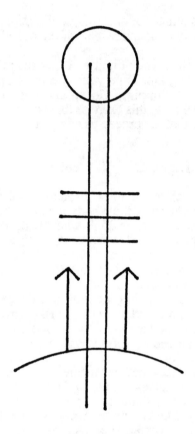

HABIT TRANSFORMING DIAGRAM

FOR ALCOHOL

Stones to Replace Alcohol

Try the following crystal exercise if you're addicted to alcohol or dependent on it and want to break the pattern; or if you're abstinent from it but want to stimulate those aspects of your consciousness that alcohol did. You'll need a chunk of citrine about half the size of your thumb and a piece of celestite about the same size. Hold the citrine in your right hand and the celestite in your left. Feel their energy spread through your arms into your chest, legs, and head. Feel it spiral through you and radiate warmth.

Essences to Repair the Damage Done by Alcohol

Hypoglycemia often results from long-term alcohol abuse. APRICOT and BANANA are each useful for hypoglycemia, but you would want to test which one is useful for you. In general, however, it is instructive to note that bananas are shaped more like male sex organs and apricots like female ones.

Essences for the heart center are very important for alcoholics, families of alcoholics, and all who love them. The best of these are BLEEDING HEART, TURQUOISE, and RUBY, but you are again cautioned to test, by pendulum or muscle testing, for which ones to use at any given time, since BLEEDING HEART especially can have a difficult catharsis of emotion from old heart wounds. The remedies for alienation may also be needed, if the addiction has gone on for a long time—MARIPOSA LILY, SHOOTING STAR, or DOGWOOD.

CHAPTER EIGHT

ORGANICALLY DERIVED DRUGS: COCAINE AND HEROIN

Cocaine addicts will doubtlessly be put out to be lumped together with heroin addicts—and vice versa. How can the ultimate upper be in the same chapter with the ultimate downer? How can upper crust snorters and tooters of cocaine be compared with the people who stick heroin into their veins?

Perhaps they're right, but you've got to organize material some way. If we sorted substances into uppers and downers, then coffee drinkers would fit into the same chapter as cocaine abusers and speed freaks, since both are uppers, while sugar addicts would go along with intravenous heroin users, since both are downers.

Instead this book is organized into gradations of damage to the subtle bodies. The natural substances which are only minimally processed (coffee, tobacco, marijuana) are the least damaging, while those which are natural but with some degree of chemical processing (sugar and alcohol) come next. Cocaine and heroin fit on the dividing line between natural and synthetic, because they are greatly changed by the processing. Most damaging of all are the synthetic drugs, to be considered in the next chapter.

The History and Nature of Cocaine

The coca plant has been cultivated for hundreds of years in the highlands of the Andes Mountains of South America. The leaves, when chewed, are a mild stimulant. They are used by the inhabitants of these high altitude regions to provide a sense of excess energy in the oxygen-thinned air. In the Nineteenth Century, coca leaves were introduced to Europe. In 1866, a patent medicine made from coca leaves and kola nuts (which supplied caffeine) was introduced in the United States under the name Coca-Cola. The leaves are still used in flavoring Coca-Cola, with the cocaine removed, although the cocaine was very much a part of the drink in the beginning and part of its enormous appeal.

Cocaine is the principle active ingredient in the coca plant. It was first isolated from coca leaves in Germany in 1844. Pure isolated cocaine is many times more powerful than that ingested from chewing the leaves. In 1884, the Bavarian army began to use the isolated cocaine to help reduce fatigue in its soldiers. Sigmund Freud heard about it and tested it on himself and his friends as an antidepressant and as an aid in overcoming morphine addiction. When he saw the dependency that came from repeated usage, his initial rave reviews turned sour. Some of his vaunted psychoanalytic ideas, however, are cocaine-inspired. Perhaps the cocaine cognoscenti among our readers will be able to discover which they are.

Cocaine is legally classed as a narcotic, as a drug that numbs the senses, but it is in fact a stimulant, the most powerful of the natural stimulants. Its effect on the central nervous system is almost instantaneous: A flash of euphoria, short-lived and sweet, often repeated. The drug was touted as being harmless, the perfect drug, not so very long ago. It can be fatal and bring sudden death but even when used only occasionally has subtle side effects over time. On a physical level, repeated use of cocaine will damage the nasal passages, causing chronic congestion, and liver and kidney damage. Because it constricts the blood vessels, it slows down the flow of nutrients and oxygen to the system. On a psychological and neurological level, the side effects range from restlessness to mild paranoia to dizziness, and ultimately, to seizures.

In 1914, the Harrison Act classed cocaine as a narcotic and ended its legal career in the United States. Twenty years ago, the use of cocaine was rare. It was the king of the Bohemian drugs, used by artists, musicians, and under-class rebels. But in the Seventies, increased governmental restrictions on amphetamines gave cocaine an increased appeal. Its high street price made it the glamor drug, the elite drug. Thus, the product of high altitudes in remote regions of the world is used to get high by people trying to acclimatize themselves to the rarified atmosphere they live in. Far from their roots, far from the normal cultural expectations they grew up with, they find themselves in the higher levels of corporate structure or the top of tall buildings on Wall Street. Or, even when they do not find themselves in such rarified positions, they aspire to them.

Cocaine as a Power Tool

If you're reading this chapter, you're probably either wondering about your own use of cocaine or about someone close to you. Why do people turn to it? Why has it become THE drug of the Eighties? The entertainment world, the sports world, and the party circuit of this country have become the home of cocaine. We don't have to mention the famous names. You know them. But why do so many turn to cocaine?

Like all drugs, cocaine is a power tool. Like a saw or a hammer, it has a certain usage and works in a certain way. People who are drawn to it innately know that it can be used that way. It alters levels of consciousness, expands vision, alters moods. Cocaine can do that. But at a certain point, using a drug is like dropping a nuclear bomb. It works. It does what you want it to do. But the price of the bomb—the after-effects, the radioactive poisoning—is it worth it?

Do you use cocaine? You're probably more creative than you know what to do with. You're probably stuck in a life situation you know doesn't suit you, but you don't know how to get out of it. Or, you're in a situation that has been expansive and growth-enhancing, but now you feel the pressure to keep growing, keep expanding. And if your life on the surface looks "normal," cocaine proves that it isn't. You are on the cutting edge of our society and you know it, but you don't know what to do about it. In fact, you feel a certain hopelessness, a certain sense of frustration.

You wake up in the morning and say to yourself, "So here I am, brilliant and beautiful, and so what? Brilliant and beautiful, and working in a clothing shop or driving a cab. Or, I'm rich and famous, but so what? I knocked myself out to get here. For what? Where's the magic they told me I would find? The sense of self?"

Cocaine is good for that. When you're somewhere and want to be somewhere else. Or when you're nowhere and know that's not where you belong. Cocaine is the power tool that gives you a heightened vision of possibilities. It lets you see beyond the limits set by our society. It makes you dance longer and further into the night. It makes you sing like a goddess. But it is not real. Cocaine, in fact, is the power tool that shows you expanded dreams, not expanded life. It carries you up to the top of mountains—and drops you back down again.

Do you worry about how much coke you're using? Do you ask yourself if it's too much? Are you finding yourself having sudden mood swings, irritability? Do you need to have it at a party? Can you limit how much you use? Do you use it alone? Are you lying about it or spending more money than you can afford? If you answered yes to any of those questions, you've got a coke problem. Do you already know all this and still find yourself not stopping, as you watch your work and relationships suffer? This is a common problem with cocaine. You can see all too clearly what's going on—it IS a tool for expanded vision—and still not do anything about it. Your life becomes like a movie. And you're not in it anymore—you're just watching.

Cocaine and Sophistication

In 10,000 years, if humans persist in using drugs that are the products of chemical laboratories, then these drugs will be genetically as much a part of your natural environment as grasses and weeds. In the present, however, human bodies aren't accustomed to laboratory-produced chemicals, and there's no right use for anything from amphetamine to aspirin.

Other hard drugs are to be scrupulously avoided by those who are seeking a way of flowing within the flow of things. We aren't saying that you ought to return to living in huts and caves. What we're saying is to put your technological brilliance into perceiving reality rather than into your body. The human body is timeless and doesn't need to ingest the Twentieth Century nor to create it. For healing, there are herbal preparations, meditations, and healing techniques like acupuncture and shiatsu which work far better than any chemical compound.

Cocaine, however, has an interesting place in this movement from natural to technological, because it is a highly refined product of an organically grown substance. There are mushroom substitutes for LSD, but there's nothing quite like cocaine. Cocaine is sophisticated. The problem, however, is that the people who use it see themselves as a thrusting movement of liberating change in new directions. Instead they are less like the foot advancing into newness and more like the shoe.

Those who THINK they're in the forefront of change are really just the rubber-soled vanguard. That's the problem with sophistication. It's the splendid, glittering image of something that it isn't. Remember, wherever you see sophistication, somewhere else, but close nearby, something truly interesting is happening. Sophistication is merely the pose of newness—of knowing WHAT it is that is new. The sophisticated get lost in poses. Happier people keep finding themselves in newness because they keep finding newness in themselves. To all those users of cocaine, ask yourselves the question: are you content to be the shoe, or are you the shoe pretending to be the foot?

Cocaine, the Chakras, and the Energy Body

New drugs are created or become popular as new social skills are required by the mass culture. If we understood how to awaken our chakras, we would not need these drugs, but because that information is so distant from our conscious minds, drugs are sometimes the best tools we can come up with. Look at the comparatively recent rise in popularity of cocaine and now its more devastating off-spring, crack. Crack appears to be almost instantaneously addictive and far more violence-inducing. Who is using them and why do they want them? Why has the culture created cocaine now as a power tool? Cocaine is popular among upwardly mobile, affluent individuals, artists, theatrical figures, rock, and sports stars. It's also used by impoverished urban underclass people, but the reason they both use it is the same.

Cocaine is a powerful tool for connecting root and third eye chakras, creating grounded visions of transformation and new growth. Similarly, it brings together upper and under-class people in buying and selling networks. Part of the function of cocaine is to bring together upper and lower chakras, upper and lower classes, into new patterns of being in the world together harmoniously. But, as you all know, the chemical tool is destructive, while the intention behind it is necessary. Better to awaken these chakras on their own and use them together than to partake of these dangerous substances. The exercises in Chapter Seven will help you awaken and heal those chakras. You can join them together through meditation, weaving them together with threads of light in a color you spontaneously and intuitively choose for the need you have at the moment.

Cocaine's effect on the energy body is subliminally perceived by those who use it. People who have the impulse to arrange cocaine in a line have the right impulse, but the line is not really meant to be snorted up the nose. The LINE they are sensing is a meridian line, as in the acupuncture meridians. Cocaine and heroin produce an as yet unrecognized medicinal effect when applied externally to the meridians. However, with enough practice, simply drawing a line of light along the meridian, with the finger if necessary, can have a far more healing effect—and you don't have to rub shoulders with drug dealers to do it. Use red light for stimulating the meridian, blue light for depressing it, and white light to simply enliven it. To teach you about the meridians would go beyond the scope of this book, but those interested can read about them further.

Heroin's History and Effects

Opium, the root source of heroin, is a drug obtained from the unripe seed pods of poppy plants, which contain a mild resin that is extracted, dried, and powdered. According to the classification of substances we're using here, opium's effects and origins put it in the same category as marijuana and hashish, as naturally occurring and minimally processed substances. However, we're including it in this chapter because few today are addicted to opium, and more to its derivative, heroin.

Opium was used for centuries in Asia and then in Europe for medicinal purposes. It was used in ancient Sumer approximately 4000 B.C. It was mentioned by Homer, and its medicinal use was suggested by Hippocrates in 400 B.C. It was only in the 17th century in Asia and the 18th century in Europe that it began to be used for its psychological rather than pain-killing effects and that addiction became a problem. Opium smoking was introduced into the U.S. in the early 1800's. Injection did not become common until after the Civil War. Laudanum, a tincture of opium, was widely used in children's cough syrups at the time.

Morphine is the main active ingredient in opium. It's a highly effective and highly addictive pain killer that was first extracted in Germany in 1805. Codeine is another opium derivative. It's a less powerful narcotic, less addictive, and frequently used in pain-relieving medication and cough syrups.

Heroin is a further by-product of opium. Its secondary treatment gives it a place in this chapter along with cocaine as an organically-derived substance altered by chemical processing. Heroin is produced by treating morphine with acetic acid to create a chemical three times more powerful than morphine. It's still used in a restricted fashion as a pain killer, especially with the terminally ill. However, it's highly addictive and thus is a controlled substance, a major factor in the illegal drug trade. Methadone, a synthetic member of the opium family, will be discussed in the next chapter.

Heroin addicts are notorious for their craving for sugar. Physiologically, this comes back to the need for fuel for the body. Heroin disrupts the body metabolism massively, depressing the normal appetite. Some survival mechanism in the brain screams out for fuel, and sugar is the fastest way of getting it. On the energy body level, both sugar and heroin create root chakra movement, but in opposite directions, so the craving of sugar is an attempt to create balance in this energy movement. Thus, when addicts leave off heroin, there may be a need to use the sugar habit-transforming diagram as well, to heal any secondary addiction to sugar.

The Incarnational History of Heroin Addicts

In the chapter on reincarnation, we spoke briefly of addictions in general as intercultural incarnation bridges and of heroin specifically as a bridge between a series of lifetimes in the Orient and a first-in-a-series life in the West. The massive numbers of deaths in W.W.II and subsequent wars on Asian turf made space for many such crossovers. These people are volunteers for the intercultural exchange necessary to build a planetary civilization over the next few generations. Long-term orientals face adjustment to a rapidly-changing western culture without the background of heritage and skills, and heroin addiction is an entry-level position into western life, as it were. That's not to say that these cultural emigres don't have a heritage and important skills, for they have a rich background of eastern values and spiritual development, as well as skills we'll need in order to suvive and evolve.

Not all of the crossovers wind up addicted—many fit in without difficulty. However, some are drawn to heroin because it's at least familiar, originating in opium, and it serves to obliterate the home-sickness and the sense of a drastic uprooting. We're not saying that all heroin addicts are from the East, but large numbers are. To find out if that's true of you personally, work with the material in Chapter Two about remembering past lives.

Heroin, a Power Tool for the Powerless

Heroin is a tool for connecting one's sense of power (the solar plexus chakra) and of place (the root chakra) when those energies aren't functioning together due to emotional and environmental deprivation. As a tool, it does the work one wants it to, briefly and effectively, for only short moments of time. As the addiction increases, heroin ultimately reverses the connection, and further disconnects these two chakras. Far better to teach anyone who feels deprived of loving home and meaningful work in the world how to activate these chakras, rather than to use this chemical tool.

However, in its time and and in its way, heroin addiction has forced the normally disinterested mass culture to stare directly into the face of these problems. The crime that grows out of the heroin addict's need to support the habit stretches its hands into the pockets of those who might otherwise go about their lives complacently unaware of other people's suffering. Affluent people who refuse to see the lives of the poor are often those whose houses get broken into, a knocking on the door of their consciousness. Only when the mass culture accepts the connection between these two chakras as the certain and inalienable right of all members of this planet, will heroin addiction phase itself out of human necessity and consciousness. As we've said before, addictions come in and out of popularity in response to changing needs of the culture and to stages in the development of human consciousness. Some of the addictions already discussed are passé, but heroin and cocaine are definitely *au courant*.

As global conditions continue to deteriorate, we'll probably find that heroin addiction becomes an even greater problem before it starts to wane. As television, global satellites, and other media increase the awareness and yearning of more and more people for this chakra linkage, more and more deprived people will be drawn to heroin. Because of television and movies, people who once lived in poverty, unaware of the extent of their deprivation, are now bombarded with this information. They can no longer live in ignorance. It's going to spread to Third World countries as we do them the dubious favor of westernizing them.

The attraction to heroin isn't always the result of severe environmental deprivation. Profound emotional deprivation, emotional poverty, even in the most affluent of homes, can lead someone down the path toward this form of addiction. To the Core Self, in its nonmateriality, poverty is poverty and powerlessness is powerlessness, no matter what its source.

The body produces pus to tell us there's an underlying infection. Heroin is a sort of societal pus. It's the calling out for a Mother Theresa. But at this point in time, people like Mother Theresas seem to be about one in five billion, so it doesn't appear likely that the healing heroin use calls out for will happen soon. But in continuing to call for social change, heroin still functions as a power tool. As with all addictive sub-stances, it's not the best tool. But sometimes it's the only tool available. It can be very hard for heroin addicts to honor that, to remember that they were searching for something once, and that their searching led them to heroin. But when the initial impulse is honored, then recovering addicts can begin to open up to the healing that will make them in time the bearers of new power tools to change society. You cannot teach effectively unless you've been there. And once you've been there and are healed, you're needed to teach.

The Connection Between Heroin and Cocaine

In the most simplistic way possible, it could be said that if cocaine is an aspect of the breakup of society, then heroin is an aspect of its breakdown. We put the two together in this chapter because their effects on the subtle body are similar. But whereas cocaine lures you with the promise of raising you above the rest of society, heroin's lure is that it pulls everyone down to the same basic, hungry, needy human level.

Cocaine promises to teach by sophistication and prosperity; heroin promises to teach by opening one up to the lessons learned from suffering and poverty. But ultimately all their promises are false. Cocaine is like a film of an elegant party, while heroin is like a photo-documentary of life in a slum. Each of them tells us about life, but neither of them is real. It's easier to see heroin as a worse tool than cocaine, but, how can you measure destruction? It's easy to see heroin as a symptom of or factor in poverty, but like all power tools, the lesson of heroin is this—that something needs to be done. And the less we look at it, the less we open up to it, the greater the problem becomes.

Habit-Transforming Diagram for Organically-Derived Drugs

As noted in earlier chapters, part of releasing and healing drug habituation is to reprogram the brain wave patterns. Nowhere is this more crucial than with hard drugs which have suppressed the normal brain waves for so long as to alter them massively. The diagram shown here is the habit-transforming diagram for organically derived drugs. Force your eyes to go up between the center two parallel lines without stopping. Repeat the upward movement ten times per session, three sessions a day.

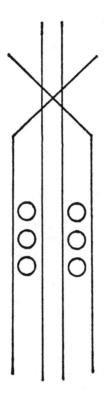

**HABIT TRANSFORMING DIAGRAM
FOR ORGANICALLY DERIVED DRUGS**

The Right Use of Organically Derived Drugs

There's no right use of chemically processed substances that involves ingestion or absorption into the human body. The human body isn't yet capable of processing these substances, any more than it's capable of digesting plastic plates. This isn't to say that these substances are entirely useless as consciousness altering tools, and what follows is a ritual which involves a minimum of four people. Four at least are needed to provide sufficient physical/electrical grounding. The members of the group use the substances not physically, which could lead to bodily damage, but instead on the mental plane. The experience is pure, detached, and free from injury, much the same as reading about a murder isn't the same as being killed.

Sit in a circle on the floor, preferably at night in a dimly lit room. Have the chemical elevated in the center of the circle, perhaps on an up-turned wastepaper basket. Have each person create their bubble of white light, then coat the surface of the bubble with blue light. Everyone together visualizes a magic circle around the group, a blue neon tube at about heart level. Breathe deeply and slowly, becoming aware of your bodies as being filled with consciousness.

Then project a tentacle of consciousness out of your body and into the substance, then back into your body again. Experience and process the consciousness-altering properties of that substance. This tentacle of consciousness can leave your body through any one of the chakras, through several, or all in succession. Some may choose to have this selection happen spontaneously, and at other times may choose to direct the process. If the energy leaves through the heart, the experience will be different than if it leaves through the brow or solar plexus. In a particular session, one could focus on a particular problem, say loving, by using the related chakra.

As with all rituals, when this one comes to its natural end, don't forget to dissolve the ring of light and your individual bubbles. This ritual should be done no more than once-a-year, and the best occasion would probably be the birthday of someone in the circle.

EXERCISE: A Light Substitute for Organically Derived Drugs

People who are dependent on organically derived drugs are seekers after something that doesn't yet exist, something new and undiscovered, whether in the world or in their own consciousness. In many parts of the world, there are religious rituals involving such substances to inspire vision or hallucination. (We refer you to the *Don Juan* books by Carlos Castenada, from Pocket Books.) The following exercise is designed to do the same, with repeated use and extreme patience, sitting like a Zen monk and doing it over and over again.

Here are the steps you take:

Sit in your bubble of white light. Feel the safety and protection of the bubble.

When you're comfortable inside it, see yourself floating out in your bubble, out on the surface of a deep, dark, endless sea.

The place you're entering is completely unknown. No one has ever seen this place before. There's no light here at all, no light except the light glowing in your bubble.

Things will pass you in the semi-darkness. Some will be beautiful, others will be ghastly. Remember that whatever you see isn't real in the world you live in, but only in the world of the mind. If you cannot keep yourself totally calm here, you don't belong here yet. Return to where you came from, knowing nothing can hurt you that you haven't created from inside, but that you're not strong enough yet to face it. (If so, skip to the end of the exercise.)

Try to hold onto some of your perceptions. Beautiful or ghastly, they can all be future learning tools, future visions.

When you've travelled far enough, rock your body back and forth slowly, to return to it your sense of this world. Then feel the sea recede around you, and open your eyes to the physical world.

Do not do this exercise any more than once a day. Do not do this exercise for longer than three minutes at a time. Not because of harm from it, but because of the energy you can lose from being a light-bearer into unlit worlds.

As this exercise is ending, you may need to sit for a while in your bubble until the light grows strong around you and inside too, to balance things out.

Essences and Stones Useful for Drug Abusers

If you like cocaine and are ready to try a crystal substitute, try this one. You'll need to get a chunk of selenite about the size of the last two sections of your little finger, and a piece of aventurine about the same size.

Hold selenite in your left hand and the aventurine in your right. Imagine that you're inhaling energy through your palms, and draw the energy up into your head. Let it drift down from there until it fills your entire body, floating through it like little bits of glowing light.

For those who've used heroin at any time, there's a need to clear out the brain wave alteration. Because the effect is the polar opposite of cocaine, do the same exercise but reverse the pattern and put aventurine in the left hand and selenite in the right.

Essences can also help. The solar plexus ones like SUNFLOWER, for self-confidence, and GOLDENROD BUD, for owning your own power can be useful. For the root chakra and grounding, use SQUASH, CORN, and MANZANITA. For clarity and getting away from being spaced out, use OPAL and CLEMATIS.

CHAPTER NINE

MANUFACTURED DRUGS AND
THE COLLECTIVE VISION

The three most common categories of addictions to manufactured drugs are amphetamines, tranquilizers, and methadone. Women, because of their particular role in our world at this time, have the highest percentage of use and abuse of tranquilizers, very often originating as prescription drugs. Until the laws were changed, they also used and abused, again with medical collusion, diet pills as a power tool to create the thin bodies society insists they must have in order to be acceptable.

Until recently, all addictive substances were either made from naturally-occurring substances or refined from them. It's only in the past two-hundred years that the so-called active ingredients in plants and minerals were isolated and then reproduced chemically in laboratories. Sugar, heroin, and alcohol were all once prepared from plants and plant products, whereas diet pills, tranquilizers, and other such drugs are manufactured.

For millions of years, the human body has been ingesting naturally occurring substances such as alcohol, and even these can do damage to the body. It has not had time yet to learn to absorb man made chemicals, which are even more damaging. Along with the so-called active ingredients in plant products are numerous other substances, not quite as active, that are also involved in the plant's effects. These ingredients include other minerals and elements which support the body's assimilation of the product. In recreating the active ingredients in laboratories, scientists have created many powerful and useful drugs, but they have numerous side effects, some profound and some subtle. The reason is that without the support of the lesser ingredients, the body cannot process these drugs as well as they did the plant products. The missing substances are like all the little points and nicks on a key. Without them, the door won't open.

Manufactured drugs affect the physical and subtle bodies in a far more disruptive way. Their frequencies retune the body in artificial and unhealthy ways. In spite of this, these chemical products do have certain positive functions, both as medications, if they aren't abused, and on an evolutionary plane. They're signs pointing us in the direction we need to go in order to change. The more we refuse to change, the longer we deny that direction, the stronger the power tools we create will become, and the more destructive they'll be.

Chemical Drugs and the Collective Vision

Why is the epidemic of addictions happening in the world? What's going on that cultures deny themselves access to healing and to vision? How can we explain the clear necessity of terrible choices and painful experiences like addictions? What's going on when age-old power tools are repeatedly abused by countless masses of people? Some would say it's a sign of how sick we are, how debased, how corrupt, how polluted, even how unnatural we've become. Some would say all that and leave it there, grumbling about what a terrible state the world is in, how ungodly, how unholy.

Not so. When a people makes new drugs more powerfully destructive than ever seen before, it's a sign about what great, never-before-seen, pure, holy places that group of people is about to enter into. Never is fear so strong as when something great and new is about to be born. The unborn child triggers the process of labor by the release of hormones into its mother's body. Hormones are chemicals, the new drugs are chemicals, and chemicals can be abused. Everything must exist in a state of balance. What's wrong is the abuse, not the chemical.

Those who are identifiably addicts are merely the vanguard of our society's movement. What they overdo, the rest do in a lesser form. Synthetic drugs are a symptom of the time. They're everywhere—in food, aspirin, birth control pills, diet pills, in so-called medications. Anyone who takes any of these is a chemical user. A chemical user can become a chemical addict. What addicts overdo, they do because the whole of us as a people wills this. You would enter into worlds so new that you must create new forms to help you see them.

Drug addicts are the front line soldiers of this movement, the ones who scout the terrain, the ones who get shot down first. The incarnational history of numbers of drug addicts is of many lifetimes as soliders. Right now, there are more warriers in incarnation than there are wars to fight. They are used to battle conditions, living in trenches, losing limbs, using substances to deaden pain and fear, and near starvation. Life as an addict to hard drugs is a hard one, and most of us wouldn't survive it for a week, but these soldier/addicts are so used to it that it hardly seems like hardship at all. Many of the Vietnam vets who've had trouble with addictions during and since that war fall into this category.

However, for many who are addicted to synthetic drugs (and also to cocaine), the karma isn't about past lives at all but about future lives, lives so different from today that the drugs serve as a tool, however destructive, to prepare for them. Just as you could use the exercises in Chapter Two to remember your past lives, you can use them to remember future lives as well. Time is more intricate than the way we perceive it, and you can remember into the future just as you remember the past.

People who are drawn to chemical drugs aren't only or even primarily those with their own vision of the new life that is coming. They're responding to the collective vision—even to the collective decision—all human souls on this planet are preparing to put into effect. They dimly sense the push toward outward expansion into joining with all the universe in its various dimensions. People drawn to these drugs are those who subliminally grasp the quickening of this new life and are struggling to keep pace.

In response to what they perceive, they yearn to see more, to hear more, to do more. The five senses are no longer enough to encompass all that we sense is possible, nor is the sixth sense, once strong in us and now atrophied through disuse. There is a seventh and even an eighth sense in the bodies we will ultimately take off-planet with us. Yet the drugs cannot actually create those senses which do not exist except in potential form. No, they create only a mocking ghostlike semblance of them which leaves the user saddened and yearning still more, for colors beyond the spectrum we can see, for sounds beyond the wave lengths we can hear, and for sensations our language has yet to develop the capacity to describe. Similarly, sound is indescribable to those profoundly deaf from birth, color unimaginable to those born totally blind.

The Place of Chemical Drugs in this Evolution

One of the reasons we keep making new drugs is because the old ones don't work. Our evolution is now so rapid that no drug works for long. In the course of this century, we've evolved immensely. The wars, the rape of the planet, have been an indication of that evolution. Once it was more functional to be an alcoholic or an opium addict because those tools worked better than now. Alcohol doesn't work as well, doesn't get you as drunk/euphoric as it did then. Alcohol is obsolete as an answer to today's needs.

What we need, today, is to prepare to live off-world. The ancestors of the Eskimos didn't learn to live in the cold overnight, anymore than our descendants will be able to live on other planets overnight. We first need to increase the limited chemical base of substances that can be absorbed by the human body so that people can function in the radically divergent environments of the future. Substances that are manufactured here may very well appear naturally and organically on other planets. The chemists who "discover" them may be getting their inspiration through tapping into the universal unconscious. Part of the process is the gradual introduction into our bodies of artificially created substances.

In one sense, nothing however seemingly artificial can be created by humans at this stage of our development that did not at one time come from the earth. At this point, there are no unnatural substances. Everything is created from something else. For example, plastic came from petroleum that once came from forests. On other planets and in other times, this limitation on substances will not be the case, but it's true for us now. It's possible to create something out of nothing, something from thought, but not here and not yet.

For now, the introduction of manufactured substances, everything from food additives to medicines to actual addictive drugs, into the body does indeed serve an evolutionary function. However, you cannot expect the body conditioned over millions of years to develop in two or three or even four generations the capacity to make chemical absorption of manufactured substances possible. Some part of every addict knows that on some level it is important, useful, and expansive to pop pills and ingest other manufactured substances. But Rome wasn't built in a day, and the human body cannot be expected to change overnight and absorb these chemical substances without damage.

So it's important, simply, to honor the wisdom in you that knows that these chemical substances are useful. And then not use them internally. Because of the extreme absorbability of the palms of your hands, it's far more useful, in the evolutionary scheme of things, to hold uppers, downers, and other drugs in your hand than to ingest them. By holding them, you can alter your brain waves and subtle genetic structure sufficiently. After several generations of such changes, we'll begin to produce offspring whose absorption capabilities are far greater than our own. So, if you've been addicted to pills, honor the wisdom in you that recognizes their usefulness, and honor, humbly, the part of you that has a crummy sense of time. You're not your great-great-great grandchildren. Leave the pills to them.

We also live in a culture that insists on instant gratification. When it's a question of our personal vision, be it of mood, emotion, or body weight, we've found it easier to take valium or diet pills than to do the kind of inner work that would erase the cause of the problem. We deal with the symptom rather than the cause. We end up hooked on uppers and downers to change the moods we feel we've no control over. We wind up hooked on diet pills to change the weight we seem to feel we've no control over. Or we're hooked on valium or qualudes or any of the chemical substances we refer to as a unit here. They vary in composition, but not in the body's inability to handle them.

Whether our vision is societal or personal, the use of substances to deepen our experience is a key that in our drugged state we mistake for a door. It's a keyhole that we mistake for the doorway into fuller vision.

Drugs distort perception, as Alice found out so well in Wonderland, but too many of us find out in detox centers. And in these centers, they often drug us again, to "heal" us of our addiction. We're victims of a culture that values performance above perception, medication above meditation.

The Place of Synthetic Drugs in Human Evolution

There are new synthetic drugs being created in laboratories every day. Most of them have medicinal functions, but some of them do not. Most of them can become highly addictive, although hallucinogens or psychedelics usually do not. In general, they might be divided into those that depress the central nervous system—downers—and those that stimulate it—uppers. Like cocaine and heroin, manufactured drugs have a profound effect upon the chakras and the energy bodies. These effects quite clearly follow from the names that we have chosen to call them.

Downers tend to draw energy from the upper chakras in the body down to the lower ones. If you're drawn to using downers, we encourage you to do the work of opening your chakras and begin to alter your energy by working with them. You're most likely drawn to these substances because you're trying to be more rooted in your body and in the world. You may be struggling with simple daily life issues, relationships, home problems, body ailments, or may turn to these substances when those problems appear.

Uppers have the opposite effect upon the chakras, in that they will draw energy away from the lower chakras in the body to those of the upper body. If you're using these substances you're probably struggling with issues of career, work, or vocation, or using them at times when you need energy and clarity. But ultimately these substances damage the chakras and the physical body, so it's far better to learn to work with your chakras than to take any of these substances into your body.

Many people alternate their use of uppers and downers in addition to using other addictive substances. You may be taking uppers at the start of the day and downers at night to simulate the natural rhythms of the body and the cycles of the day. But the desire to function at higher energy levels than normal and then lower ones soon damages physical organs and the subtle bodies ones. And yet, in a way, all of this manipulation through chemistry is an indication of the direction human beings will be moving in naturally.

As we learn more about brain and body physiology and more about how to work with our subtle bodies, we'll evolve into a race of beings with far more edurance and far greater longevity than we can now imagine. So in a way, these manufactured drugs point the way to our future development. They're as truthful as science fiction, bits of future memory. They're stories we tell our bodies. But because we've so distanced ourselves from dreams that we think we must manifest them now and not let them evolve, we've created substances to force our bodies into a future that they're not ready for, and force our minds into memories that they may not be able to handle yet.

As dream and vision become more a part of our culture, we'll be able to live with changes first as possibilities and not try to force them into physical manifestation before their time. Organic drugs had their seasons, time of ripening, drying or fermenting. But synthetic drugs exist out of time, out of season. They have the capacity to link us to other-planetary consciousnesses, but they do it at the expense of our current planetary bodies. They help to move us to an awareness of timelessness and time out of time. But we're not yet grounded enough in our bodies and minds to be able to handle these rapid shifts that are really only previews of coming attractions.

We want instant change and know it's possible, but we haven't yet mastered the inner, spiritual tools. So we've invented pills that promise to give us that; an instant cure for colds, an instant change in appetite and body size, an instant change in moods or energy level, and they do work, but only for an instant.

Earth consciousness has been seeded by guides and visitors from many other worlds for hundreds of thousands of years. They didn't have to come in flying vehicles, they came in energy bodies, in energy vehicles. On a subtle level these visitors implanted information into our physical and subtle body genetic codes. This information exists within all of us, in something like time-released capsules. As we move through linear time, these bits of cosmic information emerge. But we've created such an unbalanced left brain culture that we're undeveloped in the right brain skills needed to balance out the in-flow of this information.

So on one hand, those people who turn to chemical drugs are working with chemical tools rather than the appropriate consciousness tools to make this information available. And on the other hand, many of the people who turn to synthetic drugs are so frightened of the emergence of this information that they're using the same chemical tools to shut it out of becoming conscious.

As with everything on this planet, opposites come together and work together. But if we blame ourselves for our imbalances rather than looking at them and growing, we'll perpetuate the imbalances. But if we see this time in our history as the movement from junior high school to high school, as growth rather than failure, then we can learn from it and grow. The rules in junior high school aren't the same as the rules in senior high school and the focus isn't the same. It's time to master new skills that will prepare us to enter the college of cosmic connection. So if the slide rule of chemical drugs once worked, it's time now to learn to use the computer of our bodies and our spiritual consciousness instead.

For long stretches of human history, the seasons followed each other in fairly regular order. Today patterns of weather are changing all over the planet due to environmental changes we have created in the last two hundred years. For generations and generations, sons and daughters followed their parents as workers, farmers, traders, with countless young women dying in childbirth and countless young men dying at war. Today there are no predictable cycles in our lives. We not only do not take up the work of our parents, but seem to reject it, and not only reject it, but make numerous vocational changes in the course of our lives. And we're dying of diseases that did not exist a generation ago.

Everything is changing on earth now, and more quickly than it ever has at any other time in human history. So is it any wonder that we turn to drugs to assist us in these changes. We use amphetamines, like Benzadrine, Dexedrine and Methedrine to stimulate us. Then we use sedatives like Seconal, Nembutal, Miltown, and valium to calm us down. We use muscle relaxants like Qualudes, and even Phencyclidine or PCP or angel dust, which was first used in the 50's as an anesthetic for animals. There's Demerol and Darvon and Methadone, which promised to cure heroin addiction in the 60's but turned out to be highly addictive itself.

It's impossible to count the number of people who are addicted to pills and diet pills that offer to help us change our appetites and our bodies. And it's impossible to count the number of people with multiple addictions to substances that all began as power tools for change. Many of these substances are legal and can be bought over the counter in drug stores. Once again we find that duality in our culture, for drugs are seen as both medical healers and cultural evils.

Many of these substances are legal, but only with a doctor's prescription. And the nature of the medical system is such that great abuse of these substances can and does happen, as we know from the media coverage of performers, politicians, and athletes. But as with the substances mentioned in the preceding chapter, some of these substances are illegal and carry with them the fearful, hateful, exploitative energy of all of those who are involved in their movement through the world. It's curious, however, that many of these drugs have far greater capacity to destroy the mind and body than those substances, yet many of them are legal. Society says that if you get it from a doctor it's okay, even if you get hooked on it, but if you buy it in the park, it's not.

Drugs seem to change these days as fast as computers. It's difficult to say what the next generation of drugs will be like. The 60's dream of chemical enlightenment seems far away now, as younger and younger people are using drugs in greater numbers and with more devastating effects. But we can be certain that the more our culture resists transformation, the more our drugs will increase in potency, effects and danger. The only way to stop drug addiction is to teach the tools of transformation from birth onwards, everything from yoga to healthy eating to meditation. But as long as our prime focus is making bombs to destroy the world another 6 or 8 times over, this transformation will not happen. So drug addiction isn't separate from politics, religion, and our day-to-day lives.

Recreational and Designer Drugs

The reason so-called recreational drugs have become so popular is because, like our work, we've also outgrown most of our play. Most social interaction is empty, most lives are empty. We have to get back to what recreation really is, which is RE-creation. Little children know how to sit in the sandbox and constantly create new worlds with extraordinary fluidity, moving from role to role and game to game. As adults, we need to find within ourselves the same capacity. Most of our games have unchangeable rules that teach us or try to teach us how to live well in a world of rules, but if we're going to evolve, we need to start creating games that spread out beyond rules into higher levels of creative order. We're bored with the old kinds of play because we've grown in consciousness to the place where we need rules less and spontaneity more.

To get an idea of what the new recreation might be like, imagine a chess game where new pieces are frequently introduced as they're needed and where the board itself expands in spirals or pathways that make use of all three dimensions or even more. Imagine a football game played with four teams moving across the same field toward four different goals. The object of the game isn't to take the ball away from your opponents, but each team is trying to give the ball to one of their opponents. The competition comes from four opposing teams, each trying to do a good deed for one of the others. Imagine the kind of adult interaction around a dinner table where a circle of good friends, instead of sharing their grievances about an unpleasant day at work, all participate in helping each other to create new patterns of behavior in a work environment.

So-called designer drugs are becoming more and more popular. Imagine group interaction that achieves the same ends of initiating new and increased states of consciousness and feelings without poisoning the body. A culture that honors the body as the prime artistic creation of the soul finds means other than chemical to make alterations in the physical structure. When you remember that the soul creates the body, you can begin to recreate it. It's interesting that we use these two words, recreational and designer to describe the most popular current drugs. Recreation is about fluidity and design is about order, and they remind us of our need to grow towards more fluid ways of living in a higher plane of cosmic order.

Chemical Drugs, the Brow Chakra, and Brain Waves

The chakra primarily affected by manufactured drugs is the third eye. When you honor your attraction toward these substances as coming from a need to awaken and further activate this chakra, you can do it spiritually rather than chemically. Living in a society which denies the existence of chakras, at a time when this awakening is vital to the further evolution of humanity, supports the less than useful reliance on manufactured substances. Unfortunately, no drug can help you to see freely what you can see through the third eye when it's awakened.

The chemical structure of drugs shapes experience just at a time when you're ready to begin to experience and explore fluid states of consciousness. The effect of the chemical mimics altered brain waves necessary for such experiences. Lights, sound, and other forms of nonchemical technology are far more effective at making these changes than are drugs. Ultimately, you can grow more naturally into such wave patterns through meditation and even fantasy. There will be an exercise later with sound to help you make this shift.

In 50 years, everyone will work on these subtle levels; everyone will channel. We are becoming more and more subtle. We will ultimately move from amethysts you can hold to amethysts on the inner level, from flower essences to simply tuning into the flowers. To make this shift, we need to work with the power tools that aren't physical, through consciousness altering meditations.

For instance, though no one can teach you how, it's possible to consciously alter your brain waves to repeat the patterns created by any substance you've been habituated to, from coffee to qualudes. With some study of your memories, and perhaps by tuning into other people, you can see or feel what those brain waves look like and tell the part of your brain that knows them all too well to simply recreate them. Some of these patterns, however, with long abuse, cause dysfunction. The exercises we have given with crystals and with habit-transforming diagrams, however, alter brain waves in ways that are positive and helpful.

Certain drugs suppress the brain waves so we can leap beyond them, jump off that particular train. You can, with practice—and no one can show you how—begin to play with your own brain waves without chemicals, learning how to move from the jagged patterns generated by our stressful living into smoother, more euphoric ones. You can even alter the brain waves of people around you, learning to synchronize with them, join with them, and then change them. This technique has implications for the healing of schizophrenics, epileptics, and others whose distress has resulted in a brain wave derailment. Dolphins do this naturally, as a form of bonding, communication, and pleasure.

One of the reasons for burnout among healers and health care workers who work with addicts (or schizophrenics and retarded people) is that, without any conscious awareness, they begin to take on and mimic the disturbed brain wave patterns of the people with whom they're working. If you work with addicted people, recovering or otherwise, you need to cleanse your aura and chakras, maybe daily, by some of the exercises taught in Chapter One. In addition, you need to shield yourself at work with a white light bubble, by wearing a crystal which you cleanse daily by soaking it overnight—and from their brain waves, perhaps by wearing a light-yarmulke which covers the brow and crown chakras. (This sort of shielding, in fact, was part of what yarmulkes were for.)

There is also a connection between synthetic drugs and our newly awakening chakra, the thymus chakra. Initially these drugs stimulate this center, but within a short time, they depress its fragile new functioning. They stimulate it on a global level, for wherever anyone takes a specific drug, it is the same chemically pure substance, whereas sugar, alcohol, and marijuana vary from field to field where their plant origins grow, from season to season, from year to year. Initially they stimulate the thymus, but in a short time they both damage the chakra and the thymus gland, inhibiting the body's immune system. All chemicals, food additives, and pollutants in our air and water adversely affect our immune system, and in the future we will probably find a greater and greater occurrence of immune deficiency illnesses.

Although some of these drugs draw energy down to the lower chakras and some pull it up, and although many of them also affect the heart chakra, because they circulate in the bloodstream and affect the heart itself, in time all synthetic chemicals damage all the chakras, preventing them from functioning individually or in concert. These substances also damage the aura and energy bodies sooner than any other addictive substances, separating the layers, which creates spaces where external energies can get stuck. They also cause irregular pulses and staccato rhythms in the flow of energy in the meridians. As a child may burn its hands in a fire years before being ready to cook with it, so too are we now getting burned from the chemicals we have created.

EXERCISE: A Sound Substitute for Synthetic Drugs

In each of the previous chapters on addictive substances we have given you a substitute tool to use to stimulate your consciousness much as the substance did. There is no right use of these chemicals, but all of us have learned from the wrong uses of all sorts of things. They exist, they are a part of our world. The following exercise is designed to stimulate the brain and mind and body in similar ways to that which synthetic drugs do. Try it if you have been using them, both as a substitute for those substances and as a healing for your use of them, for about four minutes once or twice a day.

Here are the steps you take:

Sit quietly in your bubble with your eyes closed. Become aware of your breathing.

With your lips open but your upper and lower teeth touching, begin to vibrate the back of your throat so that you are making the highest pitched EEE sound that you can make. Feel that this sound is moving in circles inside your skull, at the level of your third eye, from the front to the back of your head, until you have created a vibrating ring of sound inside.

Now shift the direction in which the sound is moving so that it moves in circles through your third eye from the top of your head down between your eyes, and then around and back under your brain to the top of your head again, creating another ring of vibration.

This time take the EEE sound and slow it down so that it isn't travelling as quickly. Draw it into your brain and feel that you can pass it back and forth between the two hemispheres of your brain so that it undulates between them as if you were juggling a ball of hot melted wax between your two hands.

Now draw the sound to a point and let it spiral and dance within your brain, awakening every part of it and vibrating it.

Slowly let the sound fade, until you cannot hear it anymore, but still feel it echoing and moving inside.

Become aware of your breathing again and when you are ready, slowly dissolve your bubble and open your eyes.

Notice the changes you may feel. Do things look or seem different? Does your body feel different? Become aware of the ways this exercise can help to retune you—not to the song a chemical sings, but to the pure and wonderful electric chant of yourself.

EXERCISE: A Light Substitute for Synthetic Drugs

People who are dependent on synthetic drugs are seekers after something that does not yet exist, something new and undiscovered, whether in the world or in their own consciousness. The following exercise is designed to do the same, with repeated use and extreme patience, sitting like a Zen monk and doing it over and over again.

Here are the steps you take:

Sit in a bubble, this time one with no light at all. Feel the safety and protection of the bubble.

When you are comfortable inside it, see yourself floating out in your bubble, out on the surface of a deep, dark, endless sea.

The place you are entering is completely unknown. No one has ever seen this place before. There is no light here at all.

Let yourself move through the darkness, using all of your senses but sight to perceive what is around you. Listen, smell, taste, feel, and make use of all your subtle senses. We depend so much on vision in our society. We over-use our eyes, which prevents us from developing our other physical senses, not to mention our subtle ones.

Things will pass you in the semi-darkness. Some will be beautiful, others will be ghastly. Remember that whatever you see is not real in this world you live in, but only in the world of the mind. If you cannot keep yourself totally calm here, you do not belong here yet. Return to where you came from, knowing nothing can hurt you that you have not created from inside yourself, and that you aren't strong enough yet to face it. (If so, skip to the end of this exercise.)

When you have travelled far enough, rock your body back and forth slowly, to return to it your sense of this world. Then feel the sea recede around you, and open your eyes to the physical world.

Do not do this any more often than once a day. Do not do this longer than three minutes at a time. Not because of harm from it, but because of the energy that you can lose from being a light-bearer into unlit worlds.

As you finish, you may need to sit for a while in your bubble until the light grows strong around you and inside too, to balance things out.

In doing this exercise you will travel to new places, but see none of them. This is a great adventure, but also a great danger, and perhaps a great waste of time. Not everything invented by humanity is of value—witness pollution, atomic waste, war, rape, and violence.

Habit-Transforming Diagram for Hard Drugs

As noted in earlier chapters, part of releasing and healing drug habituation is to reprogram the brain wave patterns. Nowhere is this more crucial than with hard drugs which have suppressed the normal brain waves for so long as to alter them massively. On the following page is reproduced the habit-transforming diagram for synthetic drugs. Force your eyes to go up between the center two parallel lines without stopping. Repeat the upward movement ten times per session, three sessions a day.

Stones Substitute for Synthetic Drugs

If you're fond of manufactured drugs and ready to stop using them, try this crystal pattern as a substitute. You'll need a piece of malachite about the size of an egg yolk and a piece of rhodochrosite that is a little smaller. Hold the malachite in your right hand and the rhodochrosite in the left. Feel their energy rise up through your arms and fill your body. Feel it move from your feet to the top of your head in waves. Let it slow down or speed up by how tight you hold onto the stones. Do this for about eight minutes.

It should be noted that stopping the use of synthetic drugs is not easy and should not be attempted alone. This book cannot replace health care, therapy, or self-help groups. What it does is to give you some additional insights into the spiritual causes of your addiction. The explanations and exercises for stopping addiction in the first book, *The Spiritual Dimensions Of Healing Addiction* would also be very helpful to you.

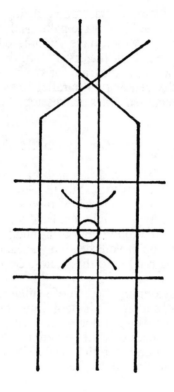

**HABIT TRANSFORMING
DIAGRAM FOR SYNTHETIC DRUGS**

CHAPTER TEN

A CONCLUSION

A person who reaches for addictive substances has been engaged for years in a ferment of visions and dream changes, none of which can manifest in the world. You cannot find an addict anywhere who is not on the brink of change and yet incapable of movement. The addict is somewhat like the Fool in the Tarot cards, about to take a giant step onto a place where there is no pavement. You live in a world of pavement, solidness beneath your feet, and all movement in your world is on these prescribed paths, roads, and highways. The person who turns to addictive substances is one who is moving outward from the dream. Such people walk not on earth but on water. The appeal of addictive substances is that they promise to make manifest the vision. What they do instead is to slowly burn away the body.

You do walk on the water, not because of your spiritual strength but because you become lighter than the water itself. You are no more than an autumn leaf cast upon the current. This body through which you were to manifest your vision is no more than a heap of dust now, an empty sack. The body is no longer channeling the vision, but merely filled with it. When you destroy the structure, the essence is wasted. You cannot put new wine in an old sack. You cannot put any wine in those who are yet afraid to make of themselves visions walking.

In *The Spiritual Dimensions Of Healing Addictions* are exercises to help those who turned to addiction because they did not know how to manifest their visions. A powerful way out of addiction is to master and direct your spiritual gifts, and we have tried to help in the exercises and processes in both books. Admittedly, these principles would help most people in our drug and sugar dependent world, but you who work with this material will be getting the first benefits.

The information in *The Spiritual Dimensions Of Healing Addictions* explained the greater reality in ways that can make it more comfortable and familiar. In this book, we also found out how substance abuse distorts the spiritual dimensions of the body and mind. Exercises and visualizations in both books help readers enhance their spiritual attunement, and use their mind power to combat both the addiction and the underlying causes.

The danger of addiction increases the more a society disowns its roots in the dream world. The growing abuse of addictive substances and other drugs in our country, by people of all ages and social groups, constitutes an epidemic of serious proportions. As you read about the spiritual dimensions of addictions, you will see that it has much to do with the spiritual condition of our culture and our loss of touch with these other levels of reality. We are in a crisis having to do with our group purpose and our group vision. To understand where addictive substances specifically fit into this, we need to take a look at human history, as we did in the various chapters dealing with specific substances.

Keeping this Book in Perspective

All physical ailments, including addiction, have long histories of mental, emotional, and spiritual imbalances that created them and that began long before the physical problem manifested. No one gets sick overnight, becomes an addict overnight—and no one gets healed overnight either.

Many people turn to alternative healing methods because they have become disillusioned by conventional medicine and conventional therapists. From the beginning we have seen the work shared in these two volumes as being an adjunct to standard health care, detoxification, and recovery programs. While your Core Self may be spiritual, if you pick up this book and think that you can heal yourself through it alone, you will be neglecting the mental, emotional, and physical aspects of who you are, and this approach will become an additional source of disillusionment.

But if you see all the available methods of healing your addiction as different aisles in a hardware store, you can wander up and down, trying out tools, finding the ones that will work best to do the particular job that you need to recover and renew your life. This book contains one set of tools, and we hope you've found them useful, but remember to pick up the other kinds when you need them—the health care, the therapies, and the self-help groups.

Addicts as Healers

This is a story that I (Andrew) have told so many times over the last few years that I cannot remember where I read it or heard it. I don't think I made it up, but in the course of telling it certain details may have changed. But anyway, an anthropologist goes off for three months to study a group of Eskimoes, in Greenland I think. He is especially interested in finding out about the native healers and their methods of healing.

In the village there is one very old man who, the anthropologist decides, must be the village healer. He spends the first month slowly courting the old man, spending time with him to gain the old man's trust. Gradually, in the second month, he begins to ask questions of the old man about healing, fishing for information the old man never provides. With only a month left the anthropologist begins to get direct, asking questions to which the man still does not respond.

Finally, with only two weeks to go, the anthropologist abandons his sense of not imposing his needs on the culture and individuals he's working with. He directly confronts the man, saying something like "You're the oldest man in the village. Everyone respects you. You must be the village healer. Why do you refuse to tell me anything about it?"

The old man looks at the anthropologist as if he is a fool. He says what to him is absolutely obvious. "How can I be a healer? I've never been wounded, and I don't have any dreams." To the old man, those were the absolute prerequisites of being a healer, and I think that they are universal.

I like to tell this story to recovering addicts, all of whom have been wounded, and most of whom have dreams. You may find, as you complete the processes in these two books, that you become interested in healing work. I think the experience of addiction and recovery provides prerequisites for becoming a healer, although my sense of what a healer is is very fluid. A chef can be a healer, and so can a gardener, a beautician, or a pianist.

BIBLIOGRAPHY

HELPFUL BOOKS ABOUT ADDICTIONS IN GENERAL

Chatlos, Calvin, M.D. *Crack: What You Should Know About The Cocaine Epidemic*. New York: Putnam, 1987.

Medical, social, psychological information that you should know about coke and crack.

The Twelve Steps For Everyone Who Really Wants Them. Compcare Publications. (See address below.)

A popularization of the twelve steps of recovery used by Alcoholics Anonymous. Valuable healing processes and spiritual growth can be gained by doing these twelve steps. Highly recommended. (Publisher has a large list of books on various addictions.)

DeRopp, Robert S. *The Master Game*. New York: Delacorte, 1968.

A classic work of the Sixties drug era, showing how to reach the same state of ecstasy and spiritual consciousness without drugs. He also wrote *Drugs and the Mind*, Delacorte, 1976.

Glasser, William. *Positive Addictions*. New York: Harper and Row, 1976.

A description of various ways to put the addictive personality to positive use. Possible helpful addictions dealt with in his book are running, meditation, chanting, and journal keeping.

Keyes, Ken. *Handbook To Higher Consciousness* Coos Bay, OR: Living Love Publications, 1975.

Author of several helpful books based on 12 Pathways to spiritual development. He talks a great deal about addiction, which he defines as programming that triggers uncomfortable emotional responses when the world does not fit your desires.

Slater, Phillip. *Wealth Addiction*. New York: E.P. Dutton, Inc., 1983

A perceptive and provocative book about the addiction to wealth that exists in our culture and the misery and destruction it creates for all of us.

Resources For Books And Treatment

Literature about A.A. and alcoholism. Alcoholics Anonymous, Box 459, New York, New York 10017. Meeting information.

Literature on alcoholism and all the addictions. Ask for catalogue. Box 2777, Minneapolis, MN 55427, Compcare Publications.

Books and pamphlets on alcoholism and addictions. An excellent source. Also a treatment facility. Hazelden Educational Services, Box 176, Center City, Minnesota 55012 (800-328-3330.)

Adult and young children of alcoholics (Groups and newsletter), NACoA, Box 421691, San Francisco, CA 94142.

Official literature and information on meetings everywhere. Overeaters Anonymous, 2190 -190th. St., Torrence, CA 90504.

Books For The Loved Ones Of Addicts

Black, Claudia. *It Will Never Happen to Me*. New York: Ballantine, 1987.

Adult and young children of alcoholics and how growing up with an alcoholic affects them. Pioneer in the field. Also did coloring book for young children called *My Dad Loves Me, My Dad has a Disease*.

Fajardo, Roque. *Helping Your Alcoholic before He or She Hits Bottom*. New York: Crown Press, 1976. (Look in your public library.)

Successful intervention techniques given, step by step. Should work for other addictions as well.

Hodgson, Harriet W. *A Parent's Survival Guide: How To Cope When Your Kid Is Using Drugs*, New York: Harper and Row, 1986.

Far more than that, this book is a clear but thorough guide to addictive substances and their effects.

Maxwell, Ruth. *Breakthrough: What To Do When Alcoholism or Chemical Dependency Hits Close To Home*, New York: Ballantine, 1986.

A tested method for intervention when your loved one doesn't want help for the addiction.

Books On Food Addictions

Bill B. *Compulsive Overeater*. Minneapolis, Compcare Publications, 1981. (See resources for address.)

An overeater's story of addiction and detailed view of recovery through the Anonymous programs. Full of wisdom.

Dufty, William. *Sugar Blues*. New York: Warner Books, 1976.

Sugar's alarming multiple effects on mind and body, including its addictive properties. Our culture's part in creating a dependency on it through advertising and putting it in foods.

Hollis, Judi, Ph.D. *Fat Is A Family Affair*. Minneapolis: Hazelden Foundation, 1985.

Ways in which family dynamics and the disease of co-dependency feed into food addictions. A very useful book in terms of making these dynamics conscious.

Orbach, Susie. *Fat Is A Feminist Issue*. New York: Berkeley Books, 1978.
A feminist perspective on the struggle women have with food and weight, seeing it as a response to women's role in society.

Overeaters Anonymous. Torrence, CA: Overeaters Anonymous Inc., 1980. (See resources for address.)

A book describing the O.A. program and the problem of compulsive overeating, with stories of people who recovered.

Rubin, Theodore. *Forever Thin*. New York: Bernard Geis Associates, 1970. (Out of print, check your public library.)

Excellent, readable picture of the psychology of overeating and the fear of being thin. His best book on the subject, but he also wrote *Alive and Fat And Thinning In America*, New York, Coward McCann, 1978.

Alcoholism Bibliography And Sources Of Information

Alcoholics Anonymous. New York: Alcoholics Anonymous,World Services Inc., 1976.

Familiarly called the Big Book by A.A. members, it gives the workings of the A.A. program and stories of alcoholics who were able to stay sober through A.A. Available at meetings, (many of which are open to the general public), the public library and the resources listed below.

Johnson, Vernon. *I'll Quit Tomorrow*. New York: Harper and Row, 1973.

A classic by a former alcoholic, who is now the founder of treatment programs, giving his own story and the typical course of the progression into alcoholism.

Jean Kirkpatrick, Ph. D. *Goodbye Hangovers, Hello Life: Self-Help For Women*. New York: Atheneum, 1986.

The special problems and concerns of the woman alcoholic are spelled out in this book by the executive director of Women for Sobriety, an alternate recovery program.

Parker, Ann E. *Astrology And Alcoholism*. York Beach, ME: Samuel Weiser Inc, 1982.

Research into the astrological charts of 100 alcoholics with some preliminary conclusions and alcoholism information.

Steiner, Claude M. *Games Alcoholics Play*. New York: Ballantine, 1971. Paperback, $2.50.

Using transactional analysis and life scripts to understand the life script of alcoholism. (Applies to other addictions as well.)

Steiner, Claude M. *Healing Alcoholism*. New York: Grove Press, 1975.

Having come a long way from his controversial first book, Steiner presents his further learning and holistic methods now in use in his California center for alcoholism.

Youcha, Geraldine. *A Dangerous Pleasure*. New York: Hawthorne Books, 1978.

Women and alcoholism, why it happens faster and is more destructive. Cultural stresses on women alcoholics.

Recommended Books On
Metaphysics And Healing

Bry, Adelaide. *Visualization: Directing The Movies Of Your Mind.* New York: Barnes and Noble, 1979.

Well-written, simple book on how to create and use visualizations to acheive your goals.

Chang, Stephen. *The Great Tao.* San Francisco, CA: Tao Publishing, 1985.

A virtual encyclopedia of information on Chinese medicine, healing, mind/body relations, energy exercises.

Gawain, Shakti. *Creative Visualization.* New York: Bantam Books, 1982.

A wonderful book with many visualization tools to use in every part of your life.   ·

Gordon, Richard. *Your Healing Hands: The Polarity Experience.* Santa Cruz, CA: Unity Press, 1978.

An excellent book on healing, it leads you through the first steps of awakening the healing power that you can begin to tap into through your hands.

Hay, Louise. *You Can Heal Your Life.* Santa Monica, CA: Hay House, 1988.

A metaphysical bestseller with a postive and practical approach, written by a metaphysician with a large following.

Joy, W. Brugh, M.D. *Joy's Way.* Los Angeles: J.P. Tarcher, 1979.

The journey of a medical doctor suffering from an incurable illness through the inner and outer stages of his becoming a spiritual healer.

Kreiger, Dolores, Ph.D., R.N. *The Therapeutic Touch: How To Use Your Hands To Help Or To Heal.* Englewood Cliffs, New Jersey: Prentice-Hall, 1979.

The person who brought healing to the medical world and made it as respectable as it can get right now has written a fine source book for apprentice healers that offers far more on aura and body healing than we could give you here.

Maltz, Maxwell. *Psychocybernetics.* N. Hollywood, CA: Wilshire Book Co. $2, paperback.

A popular classic on using positive thinking to change patterns in your life that create unhappiness.

Roberts, Jane. *The Nature Of Personal Reality.* New York: Bantam Books, 1974.

One of a series of channeled books. An exceptional book on how we shape our reality. Highly recommended but hard. Other books channeled by the same author include *The Seth Material, Adventures in Consciosness, The Nature of the Psyche, The Unknown Reality, The Individual* and *the Nature of Mass Events.* Major works available in paperback and in ordinary bookstores.

Serinus, Jason. *Psychoimmunity And The Healing Process.* Berkeley, CA: Celestial Arts, 1986.

A book on healing with channeled information, with a focus on AIDS but with valuable information for anyone who has a damaged body or immune system.

Simonton, O. Carl, M.D., Stephanie Matthews-Simonton and James L. Creighton. *Getting Well Again.* New York: Bantam, 1980.

One of the first and still one of the best books out on using visualization to heal, in this case with cancer, but valuable for anyone interested in the subject.

Useful Books On Psychic Development And Meditation

LeShan, Lawrence. *How To Meditate.* New York: Bantam Books, 1974.

A simple, useful guide to meditation, giving various techniques and step by step instructions. Written by a psychologist who has done objective, scientific research into meditation and other spiritual practices. Author of several interesting books.

Mariechild, Diane. *Mother Wit: A Feminist Guide To Psychic Development*. Freedom, California: Crossing Press, 1981.

One of the clearest and most direct books on growth, healing and expanding your consciousness.

Montgomery, Ruth. *A World Beyond*. New York: Fawcett Books, 1971.

Author of numerous books on life after death and the spiritual planes. In this one, the spirit guide is Arthur Ford, a medium and an alcoholic during his lifetime. The story of his addiction and its effects on his life after death are told in Mont-gomery's book.

Books About Crystals, Flower Remedies, and Homeopathy

Bach, Edward, M.D. and F. J. Wheeler, M.D. *The Bach Flower Remedies*. New Canaan, CT: Keats Health Books, 1979.

The original descriptions of the remedies and their purposes by the man who developed them. Not as comprehensive or understandable as Chancellor's book, but considered the Bible on the Bach remedies. (Published in the UK by C.W. Daniel, Ltd., Saffron, Walden.)

Chancellor, Dr. Phillip M. *Handbook Of The Bach Flower Remedies*. New Canaan, CT, Keats Health Books, 1971.

The best book about the Bach Flower Remedies. There are descriptions of each of the remedies with the purpose and personality traits it is designed to heal. There are case histories about each remedy, including the physical ailments of the person which cleared up as underlying emotional difficulties got better. (Published in the UK by C.W. Daniel Ltd., Saffron, Walden.)

Damian, Peter. *The Twelve Healers Of The Zodiac*. York Beach, ME: Samuel Weiser, Inc., 1986.

A treatment of the flower essences and their astrological correspondances. Donna's only complaint about this book is that she didn't write it!

Gurudas. *Flower Essences And Vibrational Healing*. Albuquerque, NM: Brotherhood of Life, 1983.

A comprehensive book on 108 flower essences, both the traditional Bach ones and the newer ones. It has interesting things to say about correspondances between the forms of plants and their healing purposes.

Gurudas. *Gem Elixirs And Vibrational Healing, Vol. I And II*. San Rafael, CA: Cassandra Press, 1985 and 1986.

Gem elixirs are made from stones in much the same way flower essences are made from plants. They tap into the healing power of stones. The two books by Gurudas are the only comprehensive treatment of the healing uses of these elixirs.

Raphael, Katrina. *Crystal Enlightenment*. New York: Aurora Press, 1985.

A fine guide to anyone starting out exploring the world of crystals and how to use them.

Dream Book List

The following are but a few of the many good books on dreams now available. Rather than describe each one individually, we will list them and suggest you look for them and others in the bookstore.

LaBerge, Stephen. *Lucid Dreaming*. New York: Ballantine, 1986.

Ullman, Montague and Zimmerman, Nan. *Working With Dreams*. New York: Dell,1985.

Garfield, Patricia. *Creative Dreaming*. New York: Ballantine, 1976.

Faraday, Ann. *The Dream Game*. New York: Harper and Row,1976.

Faraday, Ann. *Dream Power*. New York: Berkeley,1976.

Delaney, Gayle. *Living Your Dreams*. New York: Harper & Row,1981.

Williams, Stephen K. *Jungian—Senoi Dreamwork Manual*. Berkeley, CA: Journey Press, 1980.

Coxhead, David and Hiller, Susan. *Dreams: Visions Of The Night*. New York: Thames & Hudson, 1976.

Garfield, Patricia.*Your Child's Dreams*. New York: Ballantine, 1984.

Resources For Obtaining
Flower and Gem Remedies

The Edward Bach Healing Society, 461-463 Rockaway Ave., Valley Stream, N.Y. 11580

Source for obtaining the Bach flower essences.

Pegasus Products, Inc. P.O. Box 228, Boulder, Co 80306. (800-527-6104)

Source for obtaining 700 different flower essences and gem elixirs.

CPSIA information can be obtained
at www.ICGtesting.com
Printed in the USA
LVHW081338050419
613117LV00035B/707/P

9 781532 645129